Mastering

No-Limit

Hold'em

Russell Fox

Scott T. Harker

Other ConJelCo titles:

Books

Internet Poker: How to Play and Beat Online Poker Games
by Lou Krieger and Kathleen Keller Watterson

Hold'em Excellence: From *Beginner to Winner*
by Lou Krieger

More Hold'em Excellence: a Winner for Life
by Lou Krieger

Stepping Up: The Recreational Player's Guide to Beating Casino Poker
by Randy Burgess

Serious Poker
by Dan Kimberg

Video Poker—Optimum Play
by Dan Paymar

Winning Low-Limit Hold'em
by Lee Jones

Winning Omaha/8 Poker
by Mark Tenner and Lou Krieger

Software

Blackjack Trainer for the Macintosh or Windows

Ken Elliott's CrapSim for DOS

StatKing for Windows

Mastering

No-Limit

Hold'em

Russell Fox

Scott T. Harker

ConJelCo
Pittsburgh, Pennsylvania

Publisher's Cataloging-in-Publication Data

Fox, Russell
Harker, Scott T.

Mastering No-Limit Hold'em
ix,212p. ; 22cm.
ISBN-13: 978-1-886070-21-9
ISBN-10: 1-886070-21-0
I. Title.

Library of Congress Control Number: 2005924190

First Edition

1 3 5 7 9 8 6 4 2

Cover design by Melissa Hayden

ConJelCo LLC
1460 Bennington Ave
Pittsburgh, PA 15217
[412] 621-6040
http://www.conjelco.com

Table of Contents

Acknowledgements

Scott T. Harker:

This book is for my Mom. She's not a poker player, yet she taught me just as much about the game as anyone. Thank you for encouraging me to write (sorry, it's not the novel you expected) and to do things my own way.

Thanks also to my Dad, my first poker teacher. Without his assistance through life, I doubt this book would have ever had my name on it. After that first trip to Vegas all those years ago, nothing has been the same!

A very special thank you to my lovely wife Brittania and my son Blaine. You've tirelessly put up with me playing and writing, and you've given me more encouragement than you'll ever realize. I love you both!

Thanks also to my good friends Kevin Maughan, Sean McGuiness and Wes Johnson. The endless conversations about countless hands, strategies and theory have improved my game and writing immensely, and this book is better because of it. Thanks guys!

And of course, no thank you would be complete without thanking my good friend and co-author Russ Fox. Russ is one of the most patient players (and people) that I know. There are few people, if any, I respect more. Without Russ, this book would not exist.

Russell Fox:

First, thanks to my family for constantly inspiring me. Mom, Dad and Brett, when I need someone to rely on you've been there, and I lovingly appreciate it. Second, I would not be anywhere near the poker player (and writer) that I am without the zany (and highly intelligent) ARGers that I've met.

Many are now dear friends, and all have made me think and learn. Finally, without Scott this book would *never* have been completed. I owe you a debt of gratitude.

Both:

A special thank you to Michael "mickdog" Patterson for his editing efforts. His contributions greatly improved the quality of this book.

Foreword

No Limit Hold'em is a very tough game. Very tough. People ask me all the time, "What skills do I need to be a great poker player?" Invariably, they are surprised to find out that becoming a great, winning player requires only one skill:

Making Correct Decisions

At the poker table, you'll face at least one decision on every hand: do you play the hand you're dealt or fold? If you decide to play, you'll have to decide to call or raise. Should you face opposition, you'll have to decide to continue after the flop. You'll have to decide if you can bluff out your opponent. You'll have to decide if your opponent is weak, or strong, or has the best or worst hand.

Winning poker isn't about reading tells. Winning poker is not about bluffing. Winning poker is not about stealing the blinds or playing tight. While all of these things contribute to winning poker, each are a subset of the real issue at the table—decision making.

In this book, my friends Scott and Russ go deep into the world of No Limit Hold'em. You'll learn, if you pay careful attention, the thought processes that great players sort through when making decisions. When reading this book, or any poker book for that matter, read it with a critical eye and an open mind. But always, always, read it with the intent of improving your decision making at the table.

There are many ways to win at this game. You can play a very tight, controlled game like "Action" Dan Harrington. In this style, you take advantage of opponents that play too many hands and invest too much money with losers. Or, you can play a loose, aggressive style like Gus Hansen. In this style, you push very marginal advantages when you have them, and you frustrate your opponents into putting too much money into the pot when drawing slim. Both are winning strategies, and there are many shades of play between.

You don't have to be the best player at the table to win. To win in cash games, you only have to be better than 1-2 bad players. Most of the money won at the table will come from these bad players. You'll steer away from the tough guys, and do your best to get involved with the people giving the money away. Russ and Scott will show you how to separate these weak players from their hard earned money.

When I first started playing this game many years ago, I was "dead money" at the table. I was the guy that would donate hundreds of dollars to the local pros. When I sat in a game, every shark in the building would instantly ask for "a table change" and try to get near me. Learning the game takes time. I became a winning player, not overnight, but over the course of a few years. I became a winning player by watching winning players, by reading the books, and by studying the game. If I had had this book on hand in my early career, I'm certain that I would have improved more rapidly. Take the advice here and apply it at the table and your bankroll will grow.

In my experience, there are four personal qualities that you must possess (or learn) to be a world class competitor in No Limit Hold'em:

- *Aggressive*. Winning at No Limit Hold'em requires an aggressive attitude at the table. Your chips and cash are your friends. Betting and raising gives you two ways to win: either you have the best hand or your opponent might fold. If you just check or call, the only way to win is to have the best hand. You can not win if you are not an aggressive player.

- *Patient.* Winning at No Limit Hold'em requires you to be patient. Waiting for playable hands, or playable *situations*, is key to building your bankroll. Investing money in losing hands is a great way to deplete your bankroll. Be patient and wait for positive equity plays.

- *Courageous.* Winning at No Limit Hold'em requires you to have tremendous courage. All great players have "heart." What is heart? The ability to put a lot of money into the pot without the immortal nuts. Anyone can make a big bet or raise with the best hand possible, but only the great players in the world can decide to put all the money into the pot with a weak hand when it's right to do so.

- *Observant.* Winning at No Limit Hold'em requires you to be observant. Your opponents will be giving away information at every decision point. If you're observant, you'll find some tells and you'll uncover winning situations that you might have missed had your attention strayed. When you're at the table, focus on poker and your opponents and you'll find information easily available that will help you in your decision making process.

No Limit Hold'em is tough, very tough. Picking up this book and reading it, devouring it, and applying the lessons herein to your game was a correct decision. You're on your way to winning, and winning big. If you come to the table and I'm sitting there, I would very much appreciate it if you'd let me know that you've read this book—I'll need to know immediately that you'll be a winning, solid player. Good luck and have fun.

See you at the tables,

Phil Gordon
Two time *World Poker Tour* event winner,
co-host of the *Celebrity Poker Showdown, and*
author of *Poker: The Real Deal* (Simon & Schuster, 2004)

Chapter 1

Introduction

Since 2003, poker has exploded across the country (and the globe). With the *World Poker Tour* being televised every week, combined with the expanded coverage of the *World Series of Poker*, the nation's interest in this pastime has grown to record levels. This influx of new players, mostly curious beginners, has made the game extremely profitable for the knowledgeable and experienced player. And most of these players are playing no-limit Texas hold'em. For this reason alone, you should consider playing today's small cash-game no-limit hold'em: there's a lot of money to be made. These games, with fixed buy-ins of $100 or $200, or a buy-in range of $100 to $500 (or a variation thereof), are quite lucrative. Many of the players in these games have no concept of correct strategy. *Many are literally throwing their money away!* This book shows you how to profit from these players.

These games should not be played the same way as limit hold'em. They're also different from no-limit hold'em tournaments. Correct strategy draws from reading your opponents, knowing the math of the situations you will run into, and acting based on psychological factors.

No-limit hold'em is a much more complex game than limit hold'em. It requires a balance of math, psychology and intuition. Your ability to read players is paramount in this game, as instead of costing you just a bet or two, one wrong move can send you to the rail. But before you become too excited about the prospect of laying a huge bluff on your unsuspecting foe across the felt, you need to realize that the bluff is no longer king of today's no-limit games.

1

As recently as five years ago, no-limit hold'em games began appearing in online card rooms. The games attracted limit players with Doyle Brunson's famous maxim ringing in their ears, " . . . No-Limit Hold'em which, in my opinion is the Cadillac of Poker games."[1] But these players, so used to playing limit poker, added a new dimension never seen in no-limit hold'em. In short, they called everything. Bluffs no longer worked as they once did in the days of Doyle, Chip, Sailor, Slim and the road games. The skillful player had to adapt. However, in the games with a larger blind structure ($5/$10 and up) and unlimited buy-ins, the older, creative method of play can still be very effective.

This trend has continued to the present day. New players, borne out of the age of poker on television, have developed many bad habits. They play extremely loose, call large pre-flop raises with hands that would normally be considered un-playable, and even call off whole stacks with hands no better than third pair. Bluffing is no longer the big gun it used to be in these new, smaller-stakes games.

This book is geared toward these small buy-in, small blind games, and the new breed of players inhabiting them. By following the strategy that we recommend in the subsequent chapters, you too can become a winning player in these profitable games.

What We Assume About You

We assume that you have some poker knowledge, and are most likely an experienced limit hold'em player. Perhaps you've played online, and maybe you've had some success. You've probably read a book or two on the game, and per-haps you're even a winning player. You may play in a no-

---

1. Brunson, *Doyle. Super/System: A Course in Power Poker.* Las Ve-gas: B & G Publishing Co., Inc., 1994, p.419.

limit game at your local card room or favorite online site, and now you have decided to really learn the game. You sense that there is a lot of profit to be made in these games—and you're right!

We also assume that you're prepared to put forth the effort and hard work it takes to become an exceptional player. Buying this book was the first step, and if you've come this far, we'll assume you're going to go all the way. You've chosen this book because you understand that changes in the game require changes in strategy. We intend to teach you that strategy in the pages that follow.

What You Will Learn

In Chapter 2, we will introduce you to all of the important cardroom rules, as well as the many faces of no-limit hold'em. We'll talk about new games, long-running games, big stacks, small stacks, passive players, maniacs, and even what to do if you find yourself as the short-stack at the table.

In Chapter 3, we'll discuss the fine art of knowing your opponents. While important in limit poker, this skill is even more critical in no-limit poker, as your whole stack is at risk on any given hand. The more you know about your opponents, the better you will play against them.

Chapter 4 addresses odds and betting strategies. Most of your decisions will be based on knowing your opponents (psychology) and odds. In this chapter, we teach you about pot odds, implied odds, reverse implied odds, and how they affect your play. We'll also discuss the proper amounts to bet, why you bet those amounts, and when to do so.

Chapter 5 is all about position. We'll teach you what hands to play from each position in the seven different situations you will face. No-limit hold'em is very situational, and we investigate pre-flop situations to determine the proper move.

We'll also discuss the important topic of how to play while in the blinds in Chapter 6.

Have you ever thought about playing draws in no-limit hold'em? In Chapter 7, we'll discuss draws, when you play them, and when to avoid them. Contrary to what you might have heard, draws can be very profitable in this game, and we'll show you how to get the most out of them. We then examine flop play, looking at most of the situations you will encounter.

Chapter 8 continues our play topics with the play of the turn and the river. These are often neglected in poker literature, but we take a hard look at the confrontations you will face in these betting rounds. We also discuss a few special plays.

Chapter 9 explains the house rake, what it is, and why you need to be concerned. You might be surprised to find that, because of the rake practices, some no-limit games are virtually unplayable.

In Chapters 10 and 11, we shift to the more personal side of the game. Two topics seldom written about are management of yourself and of your game. We'll teach you how to avoid tilt, when not to play poker, and how to maintain the best balance of physical and mental states to make you a winning player. After that, we tell you how to make the most out of your time away from the table, including what (and how) to read, where to discuss poker, and how to manage your results and your bankroll.

After the concluding Chapter 12, we've written a useful and challenging quiz to test your knowledge. We're sure you will have learned a lot by the end of the book, but take the quiz anyway, just to make sure.

As an added bonus, we've included a complete summary of an actual eight-hour session of no-limit hold'em played by one of your authors. It is our hope that you will have a much better idea of what to expect if you follow our guidelines for play. You'll note that most of the hands are folded before the flop. Get used to that. One unknown player once described no-limit hold'em as "hours of complete boredom broken up by moments of sheer terror,"[2] and we believe that is pretty accurate. You'll find this session summary in Appendix A.

Appendix B lists references to many of the books we mention in the text, as well as a recommended reading list. There are a lot of great books out there, and we'll tell you which ones we feel are the most worthwhile.

Appendix C contains a few starting hand charts based on the recommendations in this book. Unlike hand charts in other poker books, these give you suggestions based on position, the action to you, and your knowledge of the current game conditions you face.

Finally, Appendix D is our glossary. Many terms in this book will be familiar to you, but some might be new, so look them up!

Conventions and Notation

Throughout this book, there are certain conventions that you should be aware of. There will be new terms introduced in the text. These terms will be in *italics* and will include a brief definition. The glossary in Appendix D defines these more thoroughly.

Hands will be notated by the value of each card 7, 9, 3, etc. Face cards will be denoted by a capital letter A (ace), K (king) and so on. Most of the hand notation will also include the suit ♥, ♠, ♦, ♣, such as A♥Q♦. If there is no suit, we will

---

2. The original author is unknown, although this quote appears in many books and articles.

use a small "s" to denote a suited hand, and a small "o" for an unsuited hand. For example, "KJs" is the notation for king-jack suited, and "AKo" is the notation for ace-king off-suit. Some hands, when the suits are irrelevant, will be written without an "o" or an "s." For example, "QT" means any queen-ten, and "86" means any eight-six.

One Final Thought

As poker players, we learn something new about the game nearly every day. As you read books and play, you will intuitively pick up more and more information, technique and understanding of this amazingly complex and fascinating game. We encourage you to not only read this book, but to study it. A good poker book can be used as a reference and a refresher for years and years. It is our sincere hope that this book will do the same for you.

Finally, if you have as much fun reading this book as we did writing it, our mission is complete. Poker can be a fun and profitable hobby (and sometimes profession), and we hope the lessons in this book will pay for themselves many times over as you apply them at the poker table. Good luck!

Chapter 2

The Many Faces of No-Limit Hold'Em

I t seems that all low-limit no-limit hold'em games are the same. You can do the same things no matter what the stacks are, no matter who you are up against, regardless of your image. If only it were that easy.

The reality is quite different. There is a *huge* difference between playing in a brand new fixed buy-in game where everyone has the same chip stack, and playing in a game that has gone all night where your chip stack is one fifth the size of the *average* stack and one *fifteenth* the size of the largest stack. If you have a tight image you can make plays that a player with a loose image should not make (and vice versa). The size of the blinds is yet another factor that impacts your play. These are just some of the things you must consider when you sit down to play in a no-limit hold'em game.

The House Rules

The title of this section has a double meaning. The house (the cardroom or casino) rules the roost: it is saddled with the responsibility to run an honest, fair game (and takes a "tax" from each player as a result). The cardroom also must enforce certain house rules that are consistent across all the tables of a particular game. Knowing *how* the house rules, and *what* the rules are, gives you that feeling of certainty and confidence you want to project when you first sit down in a no-limit game.

Fixed vs. Variable Buy-in

Every cardroom differs in the kind of no-limit hold'em games offered. Some offer *fixed* buy-in games while others allow a range (or *variable*) of buy-ins. In a fixed buy-in game, you *must* buy-in for a specific amount (usually $100 or $200). Casinos and cardrooms offering these games include the Bellagio in Las Vegas and most Southern California cardrooms. In contrast, some cardrooms offer games with different minimum and maximum buy-ins. For example, the Mirage in Las Vegas allows players to buy-in for between $200 and $500. Most online sites follow this procedure. In all cases, we recommend you buy-in for the maximum possible amount—there is no reason to put yourself at a disadvantage with your opponents by buying-in for a smaller amount.

Rebuy Options

Each cardroom has different options regarding when you can make a rebuy. Most online sites allow you to rebuy up to the maximum buy-in at any time. However, the rules vary greatly in brick and mortar cardrooms. For example, in the $100 fixed buy-in game at the Bicycle Casino in Los Angeles, you can rebuy an additional $100 in chips whenever you are at $50 in chips (or less). You are also allowed to do one short rebuy (after each short rebuy, you must make a full rebuy). Thus, if you fall to $20 in chips, you can take a short rebuy of $30 (bringing you to $50) and, on the next hand, make a $100 rebuy bringing you to a total of $150 in chips. Also, if you lose all of your chips, you may rebuy $150 in chips. In contrast, the Commerce Casino only allows rebuys of $100 in chips.

Whenever you play in a cardroom for the first time, make sure you know what the rules are regarding rebuys. Ask the floorman for the specific rules; he will be happy to tell you what they are and when you are allowed to make rebuys.

House Money: Rakes and Jackpots

Cardrooms are businesses set up to make a profit. To cover their expenses and make money for their shareholders, they charge a small fee (rake or time charge) to play in the games they run. Additionally, many cardrooms offer bad-beat jack-pots. We discuss both of these important subjects at length in Chapter 9. For now, note that the rake and jackpot drops at all cardrooms may differ, especially in competitive situations.

Nine-Handed versus Ten-Handed

Games in California are almost always nine-handed. Games in Nevada are almost always ten-handed. In hold'em, only two additional cards are dealt out—not much changes, right? Actually, for hold'em that is usually the case.

Ten-handed games are slower games than nine-handed games. First, an additional hand must be dealt and an additional action (bet, call, or fold) must occur. While this does not seem like it would impact the game much, it does slow the game down a bit. For whatever reason, slower games (i.e. the physical speed of dealing and betting) tend to be tighter games. We don't know the reason why, but we have observed this effect for years.

Overall, there just is not that much of a difference between nine-handed and ten-handed games. You do have to be slightly more careful from early position in a ten-handed game (there is one additional opponent out against you). And if you normally play nine-handed games you may find the ten-handed game slightly tighter than you are used to.

The Blinds

When you play restricted buy-in no-limit hold'em, the blinds vary depending on the casino. Typical blinds are $1/$2 (the first and lower number is the small blind while the second and higher number is the big blind) or $2/$3 for a $100 no-limit game and $2/$3, $2/$4, $2/$5 and $3/$5 for a $200 no-limit game.

You may be thinking that there is not much of a difference between $1/$2 and $2/$3. However, that's just not true.

Assume you play four *orbits* (an orbit is a round so that every player has held the button) and are dealt the 7♥2♣ each and every hand. In a $1/$2 game, your bad luck has cost you $12. In a $2/$3 game, you are out $20, or 67% more than in the $1/$2 game.

Tight play *tends* to occur when the blinds are smaller. Players feel that there is less of a need to play hands. After all, it is only costing them $3 an orbit. If you combine $1/$2 blinds with a ten-handed game (see *Nine-Handed versus Ten-Handed*, above) and knowledgeable players, you can easily get a tight no-limit game. Additionally, blind stealing becomes less relevant as the blinds shrink. Blind stealing is almost non existent in a $1/$2 blind structure.

Contrast that with the standard California game with $2/$3 blinds. A tight player might sit out four orbits and find that 20% of his starting stack has vanished. This can cause players to seek action, to make moves that they should not; in other words, the higher blinds can lead to a faster game. It does not always work that way, but it can.

Consider, too, the ratio of the blinds to your starting stack. In a $1/$2 blinds $100 game, your starting stack can survive 33 orbits. However, with $2/$3 blinds you can only survive 20 orbits. If your starting ratio of stack size to blinds is 30 to 1 or higher, your stack size is comfortable. However, if it is less than 25 to 1, you are short-stacked. Consider a typical progression in a hand in a $2/$3 game. The big blind is $3. The first raise is to $15. The second raise is to $40. The third raise is, well—it is all-in! Are you going to raise to $90 leaving yourself with $10? Now take the same progression in a $1/$2 game. The first raise is to $10. The second raise is to $25. The third raise is to $60. Yes, the raise to $60 leaves you short-stacked (with $40); however, re-raising to $100 would be too large of a raise.

When You First Sit Down at a Table

Janus, the Roman god of gates and doors, had two faces. In no-limit hold'em, we have to consider not two faces but *multiple* faces. It's one of the reasons why playing no-limit can be a different experience each time and why it can be so frustrating. Here are some of the major facets you need to consider.

When the floorman (or other casino/cardroom personnel) seats you at a no-limit table, you need to make a number of observations:

- Is this a new game?
- Do you know how any of your opponents play?
- What are the chip stacks of your opponents?
- Is there a standard raise?
- How are your opponents playing? Passively or aggressively?
- Are there any maniacs at your table?

Let's examine each of these issues in sequence.

Brand New Games

Many of the variables of fixed buy-in no-limit hold'em games go out the window when you sit in a brand new game. Everyone has the same number of chips. Unless you know some of your opponents, you have no idea of how they play. You and your opponents are groping in the dark.

Some no-limit games have a buy-in range. For example, the game at the Mirage in Las Vegas allows you to buy in for between $200 and $500. Here you must decide your buy-in amount. We strongly recommend you buy-in for the maximum amount. First, many of your opponents will buy-in for the maximum. Second, if you purchase the minimum number of chips you will be relatively short-stacked. Say you buy

$200 in chips. Why put yourself at a disadvantage when you don't have to? Of course, if you cannot afford the game, you should not play in it.

Once you sit down in *any* new game you need to observe, observe, and observe some more. How else can you determine how your opponents are playing? Your goal should be making money, not knowing how the Bears are doing. If you can watch the football game and your opponents at the same time, well, you have much better observation skills than we do.

How Your Opponents Play

Usually when we sit down in a game we know one or two of our opponents. If we know two people in the game, that means we know 25% of our opposition. Some of the time we don't know anyone in the game. When that happens we must—for the first few orbits—observe our opponents to determine how they play.

During the first couple of orbits you want to learn how your opponents play, so when you are involved in a pot with them you will have a better idea of what to do. This does not mean that you should fold your playable hands. Rather, you should play normally: betting your good hands and folding your bad ones.

Chip Stacks

In a brand new game, everyone starts with the same number of chips. Much of the time you will find yourself placed in a game that has been going for some time. Look at the chip stacks at your table. With your initial buy-in are you short-stacked or about average? What is the standard initial raise at your table?

Let's assume that you sit down in a $100 fixed buy-in no-limit hold'em game that has been going for some time. As you look at the other eight players, you note their approximate chip stacks: $85, $140, $100, $225, $30, $150, $130, and $500. Although one player has you significantly out-chipped, your stack is only slightly below the average of the other seven players. No special adjustments are required.

However, consider these chip stacks that one of the authors faced when he sat in a $100 fixed buy-in game that had gone all night: $450, $1300, $320, $1400, $400, $800, $80, and $750. In this instance the chip stacks of the other players ensured that the author was short-stacked. Special adjustments (discussed below) were required.

After you've been in a game for some time, you will (hope-fully) become a big stack. There are plays you can make with a big stack that you cannot make with a small stack. We dis-cuss some of these opportunities later in this chapter.

The Standard Raise

Assume you sit down in a $100 fixed buy-in no-limit game with blinds of $2 and $3 that has just been started. As the chip run-ner gets your chips, you watch the action. A couple players fold, and from middle position Ralph makes it $12. On the next hand you notice that Alice raises on the button to $12. Five minutes of observation show that most players are raising to $12—it's the table's de facto standard raise. You notice that your friend got seated in another $100 $2/$3 blinds no-limit game at the next table. He mutters to you, "I can't believe it. These guys have a standard raise to $27! After playing all night, can't they go home?" Two games with the same rules separat-ed by five feet. Yet these games will play *very* differently.

In general, the more chips on the table, the larger the stan-dard raise. Players feel the psychological need to make larg-er raises because of the larger number of chips on the table. And, in general, it is the correct conclusion (although drawn by the wrong reason).

Assume Joe has started with $100 and has grown his stack to $200. Joe is not likely to change his game; doubling his stack size is a typical goal of players. Two hours later Joe has grown his stack size to $450. Joe undoubtedly feels quite good. He probably does not want to drop back to $200; however, he's likely to risk $100 on a hand that normally he'd avoid. Now assume that Joe has played all night and has moved his stack all the way up to $1100. It is almost a certainty that Joe will be playing "fast and loose" relative to his *normal* standards of behavior. Of course, if Joe is an *über-tight* (tighter than what most players consider tight) player, his "fast and loose" may look like some players tight play!

The authors have done the same thing. Take a look at hand 184 of the sample session on page 176 in Appendix A. The author held AQo with a large stack ($497) in middle position and raised to $15. A player who had previously overbet a 98s re-raised all-in to $81. The author called—a clear mistake.[3] The other player is unlikely to hold something so weak as a 98s (and even then the 98s is only a 1.42 to 1 underdog). A factor that the author considered on a subconscious basis was that he could *afford* to lose that $66 because he was a substantial winner on the day. After that hand, though, $66 of his winnings had needlessly vaporized.

How Are Your Opponents Playing?

As you observe your opponents, note how they are playing. Are they tired? Are they drinking? Are they playing aggressively or passively? Are they on tilt? After just a few orbits you should be able to judge the style of your opponents.

---

3. It's a mistake to call the additional $66 because at best it's a coin-toss situation. At worst, the author is dominated. Calling $66 to win $96 when you have pot odds to make the call *only* when you're in the best case, coin-toss situation is not smart poker.

If a game has been going all night, it is likely you will be playing against players who are tired. We strongly recommend that when you get tired you cash out—you lose approximately 25% of your higher-level cognitive capacity with each 24 hours of sleep loss.[4] Studies indicate that just 18 to 21 continuous hours without sleep lead to performance impairments similar to those seen with blood alcohol levels of 0.05% to 0.08% (a level that is considered legally intoxicated in most jurisdictions).[5]

Many of your opponents will be tired and/or drunk. Their reaction times will suffer, they will make incorrect judgments, and they may be overly aggressive or passive. Whatever the impact, they will not be playing their normal game.

We have found that the most noticeable tendency of tired players is for them to make bad decisions. They will call when they should fold, they will raise when they should fold, and they will fold when they should call or raise. This makes acting against such players difficult because you can't trust their actions to help you decide what they hold. We recommend straightforward poker against such individuals by betting your good hands and folding your bad hands.

We should point out that a few individuals supposedly play better when inebriated than sober. While scientists might

---

4. Balkin, T., G. Belenky, J. Leu, D.M. Penetar, K. Popp, D. Redmond, H. Sing, M. Thomas, D. Thorne, and N. Wesensten. "The Effects of Sleep Deprivation on Performance During Continuous Combat Operations." *Food Components to Enhance Performance*. Washington, DC: National Academy Press, 1994, pp. 127-135. This book is available online at http://www.nap.edu/books/030905088X/html/.

5. Arnedt, J.T., A.W. MacLean, P.W. Munt, and G.L.S. Milde. "How do Prolonged Wakefulness and Alcohol Compare in the Decrements They Produce on a Simulated Driving Task?" *Accident Analysis and Prevention*, (2001), 33:337-344. See also, Dawson, D. and K. Reid. "Fatigue, Alcohol and Performance Impairment." *Nature*, (1997), 388: 235.

dispute this, we look at them as the exceptions that prove the rule. *Most* players will not play as well when tired or drunk. If you run across someone who is an exception to this, make a note of him.

When you run into players playing overly aggressive, you should adopt the opposite strategy: playing tight. You can't *run over* them (force them out of the pot with large bets), so let them run over themselves. Suppose you hold T♠T♣ and have called an aggressive player's pre-flop raise and flop a set. Let the aggressive player do the betting for you—he will almost always hand you more chips than you could get by betting yourself! The check-raise is a potent weapon to use against these players.

If you're up against an aggressive player who likes to steal the blinds, consider playing back against him when you hold a reasonable hand in the blinds. Say you hold K♦T♦ in the big blind. An aggressive player who has raised your last seven big blinds again raises. Your hand is good enough to raise him back. You need to try to tone down your aggressive opponent's behavior. Be aware that your opponent can hold good cards—everyone gets the same cards (including pocket aces) at the same frequency in the long run.

You *can* run over opponents that are too passive (but not calling stations). Bet or raise with your marginal hands because you are likely to win the pot. These opponents are looking for ways to fold their hands. Give them a reason to do so by raising. However, if a very passive opponent bets or raises strongly, it is likely he has an excellent hand.

When a player is on tilt, he will consistently make bad decisions. He will give his money away. It is hard, though, to force him to give his money to you. You will need a good hand to play because most players on tilt are involved in too many hands. Your other opponents will, most likely, be aware of a player being on tilt (it's usually obvious even to the unobservant) so it is hard to isolate him.

Is There a Maniac at the Table?

Maniacs are not aggressive; rather, they are *extremely* aggressive. They play far too many hands (even more than a typical aggressive player) and bet and raise too much. They do not respect other players' bets and will typically call most opponents' raises. You will be forced to make decisions for most of your chips. Maniacs increase your expected winnings but at the cost of increased variance.

We suggest tight, straightforward play against a maniac. Like aggressive players, maniacs will bet for you. When there is a maniac at the table, just sit back and enjoy the ride. Your poker session is about to emulate a roller coaster. You can also be more confident in your big hands against a player like this who will overvalue or overplay just about any two cards he is dealt.

Plays You Can Make with a Small Stack

When you have a small stack the plays you can make are limited. You are more likely to be a target of the big stacks—in general, they will try to bet *you* off hands. Like a small stack in a tournament, you must pick and choose your spots carefully. This does not mean that you should sit back and blind yourself off into oblivion. In poker, the aggressive bird gets the worm (so to speak). So how can you be aggressive with a small stack?

First, because you are being selective, you will (for the aware players at your table) have a tight image. To a small degree this counterbalances the impact of your small stack size. Your raises will be noticed. Unfortunately, because you won't have many chips in back of your raises, this may not be enough.

An effective strategy is to raise all-in with any hand you wish to play. If you have an acting streak, *this* is when to use it. As you move your chips in, either look resigned to your fate or mumble (but loud enough for the table to hear), "I can always rebuy" or "Might as well shove 'em in." Of course, you have a premium hand so the actual statement should be, "I can always rebuy *if my premium hand loses*" or "Might as well shove 'em in *to double up*."

An important point is that you should *raise* all-in, not call all-in (unless you have aces or kings). When you are the aggressor, three things can happen, and two of them are good:[6] your opponents may fold (and you win the hand then and there), you are called in one or more spots and win the hand, or you lose the hand. When you call all-in you either win or lose the hand. It is far superior in no-limit to be the aggressor, especially when short-stacked.

A second strategy that can be used is to play some very marginal hands in late position when there are a large number of callers hoping to hit the flop. Let's look at an example. You have $60 (having just lost a big pot) in a $100 fixed buy-in $2/$3 blind no-limit game. You look down at 9♦7♥ in the cut-off position. An early position player raises to $7 and four players call. Normally you would fold this hand but in this situation you might elect to call. It is likely your cards are live. If you hit the flop you can win a large pot. You should glance at the button and the blinds to see if they show any signs of re-raising (if they do, you should fold). If you miss the flop you can fold. An important factor behind this strategy is that in most $100 fixed buy-in no-limit games, you can rebuy when your stack is down to $50. Of course, with a better hand (e.g. 9♦8♦) either this play or re-raising all-in are the clear options.

---

6. With apologies to Woody Hayes. See page 59 in Chapter 5.

Remember, stack size leads to intimidation against *aware* opponents. However, advanced plays work only against those who recognize them. If you are up against the *unaware*, play normally. Your lack of chips will not be a factor they will consider.

When You Have a Big Stack

You have options when you have a big stack. You can see more flops, you can raise more often, you can tighten up or you can play your normal game. We'll examine the pros and cons of each of these strategies.

The goal of seeing more flops (by calling limps and/or limping on hands you would normally fold) is to hit more flops at a low cost. For example, suppose you hold T♦9♣ in middle position, a hand that we believe should be folded. Suppose someone has limped ahead of you. If you have a big stack, why not invest the cost of the big blind on the chance that you'll hit the flop? Ideally, you'd like a flop such as J♣8♥7♦, T♥9♦2♠, or 9♠9♥5♦.

Now you may be asking why we don't normally recommend you play a hand like T♦9♣ with a limper. Statistically, you are more likely to lose money when you play this hand (even for just the cost of the big blind). You may be raised (and you'll have to give up the hand), you may hit one pair (and likely either be unable to bet or lose money to one pair with a better kicker), or you may miss the flop. These tend to happen far more frequently than the times when you hit the flop, bet, and win money with the hand.

But when you have a large stack you can *occasionally* play these hands. Some of your opponents will be fearful of your large stack and will back off from raising when they should raise. However, if you have a maniac left to act you should not even consider playing hands like T♦9♣ (the chances of a maniac considering your stack size is negligible). We don't recommend you use this play every time you hold a hand like T♦9♣ because playing these cards is likely still a slightly negative *EV* situation.

A second strategy to consider when holding a big stack is raising more often. This does not mean making your standard raise larger; rather, you should consider raising with hands that you would normally just call with. This strategy succeeds against opponents who are intimidated by large stacks (the weak-tight players and those generally fearful of losing their stack). The risk is that even the fearful and weak-tight players hold good hands (and at the same frequency as us). Overall, this strategy works and will increase your winnings. It should be noted that this strategy does not work against maniacs and opponents who hold large stacks. Your raises will not intimidate them.

A third possible strategy is to tighten up your play with the goal of preserving your win. Players who choose this strategy (and we have seen this strategy used) miss opportunities to increase their winnings. If you want to preserve your win then the best maneuver is to rack up your chips and leave the game. If you elect to continue to play, why not take the actions that likely will increase your winnings? Of course there is a risk involved (you always have the potential of losing your winnings). However, poker *is* a form of gambling. If you are fearful, your chances of winning fall considerably.

A fourth potential strategy is to just play your normal game. The moves you make will be the same as if you had an average stack. While this strategy is far superior to the preservation strategy, we believe that you can increase your winnings by, at a minimum, using stack-size intimidation moves. If you've got it, flaunt it!

Big Stack as a Weapon

Our concluding thought for this chapter is that you should use a big stack as a weapon. The goal in poker is to have your opponents make mistakes with their hands. Consider the following hand.

You hold 9♥9♦ two to the right of the button in a $100 fixed buy-in $2/$3 no-limit game. Two players limp and you raise to $20. Everyone else folds, but both limpers call. The flop comes A♠8♣4♥. The first limper checks (he has a stack of $70 remaining). The second limper bets $25 of his $120. What would you do? You have a stack of around $400. Unfortunately, you know nothing else about these players as they have both just joined the game.

The actual player raised all-in, representing either AA or AK. His thought process was:

> It's unlikely either of these players has a big ace because they would probably have raised or re-raised, either initially or when I raised. The bettor probably has a middle ace, something like AT or A9, perhaps with a backdoor flush draw. The $25 bet seems like a feeler bet. If he has A8 I'm putting him to a tough decision, and even if he guesses right I'll have a chance to redraw on him. My only concern with the first player is that he flopped a set. If so, I'll have redraws. The reality is that neither of these players is likely to call me.

The first limper quickly folded. The better thought for a few minutes and tossed his A♦T♦ face-up into the muck saying, "Nice hand."

If you can earn a big stack, use it. You'll garner additional profits. Isn't that why you play poker?

Chapter 3

Knowing Your Opponents

T.J. Cloutier called getting to know your opponents, "The most valuable skill in big-bet poker."[7] We couldn't agree more. You can win holding mediocre cards in no-limit poker, but it is difficult to win with those same cards in limit poker. You can capitalize on your opponent's tendencies, fears and beliefs in no-limit while in limit poker it is too easy for an opponent to throw in that one extra bet.

You have a personality: a set of beliefs that govern how you act. Psychologists tell us that our personalities are set by the time we reach thirty. If you're an extrovert at thirty, you'll be one at seventy. Likewise, most of our actions and mannerisms are also set by the time we're adults. Some people are naturally gregarious while others are closed-mouthed. It is almost impossible for people to have a completely different personality at the poker table than away from it for any length of time.

These beliefs determine not only our personalities but also our patterns of actions. For example, many people have a choice of ways of driving to their office each day; however, most of them will choose the same way day after day. Some of these people choose the means that they perceive results in the fastest trip. Others may like the scenery along a specific highway. No matter the reason, they make a rote decision.

When it comes to the poker table, your opponents likely have a set way of playing every hand. Let's take a trouble

7. T.J. Cloutier, *Championship No-Limit & Pot-Limit Hold'em*, p. 28.

hand at no-limit hold'em: 9♠9♥ from early position. Does your opponent always raise with any pair? Does he or she just call? Will the pair of nines always be tossed in the muck from early position because it is not strong enough to act?

The first time your opponent held 9♠9♥ in early position he may have raised. Let's assume he lost the pot. His brain registered that raising with pocket nines in early position doesn't work. The next time he found pocket nines in early position he folded—he wanted no part of that hand! However, the board came with a nine; he would have been a winner had he played that hand. Subconsciously he knew that folding wasn't the right action. So a few hands later the opponent again finds 9♠9♥ in early position. This time he calls and wins the pot.

A month later the same individual picks up pocket nines in early position and this time he calls. His brain tells him that's the winning action (whether it is or not is irrelevant; he *perceives* that it is and that's all that counts). Indeed, it is important to remember that people act based *on their perception of reality, not the reality itself.*

As humans, our brains rationalize patterns because we would be otherwise overwhelmed with information. If you look outside and see rain falling, you grab your umbrella. We don't have to think about it because we associate *protection from rain* with *umbrella*. Likewise, if we see a player raising from early position and we hold 7♥2♣ we fold (when it's our turn to act) without thinking; why would anyone play a dog of a hand like that against someone showing strength? This is why your opponents have betting patterns. Unfortunately, unless you recognize those patterns, knowing that they exist is useless.

Physical Actions. When your cards are dealt to you, what are you doing? Are you looking at your cards? Are you watching your opponents to see what their reactions are? Don't look at your cards until it's your turn to act; instead, watch your opponents. Many times they will give you physical signals on how they are going to act. Here are some of the common physical signals that your opponents will send:

- Reaching for chips. This almost always indicates *strength*. It usually shows that your opponent will be playing the hand.

- Complete disinterest in the hand. Normally indicates a player that will fold. There are a few players who will send this signal when they have great strength; you will need to catalog those players.

- Smiling/Frowning. In Mike Caro's *The Body Language of Poker*,[8] he notes that strength shows weakness and weakness shows strength (in physical gestures). However, that tell is now so well known that unless everyone at your table is a beginner, it is not as likely to be correct. However, many people involuntarily smile or frown when they pick up a hand. It will mean that they have either a strong or weak hand. You will need to catalog, for each player, whether a smile or a frown indicates strength or weakness.

- Nervousness. Unfortunately, there are many reasons why an opponent may be nervous when they look at a specific hand. These include a lack of knowledge on how to play the hand, a very strong hand, a marginal hand, or nervousness regarding the game.

In order to increase your success you have to categorize your opponents. Take surreptitious notes while you're at the table. Just the act of writing down that 'John looks nervous when he plays TT' will help you remember that fact. There

---

8. Caro, Mike, *The Body Language of Poker,* Chapters 12 and 13.

are a number of other good reasons to take notes; see "Taking Notes" on page 139 for more on notetaking.

Of course, to be able to utilize the physical actions of your opponents you must be observing them, not the game on the television. Here's an example of a recent hand that illustrates this. Pre-flop, an early position player made a small raise. This tended to show a small pair. A second player was on the button and held J♥J♦. He felt, correctly, a raise was warranted. However, his left-hand opponent (LHO) was counting out chips to make a raise. The LHO was the tightest player at the table, and would play a pair of tens or higher, or AK or AQ. Given that the button's hand was substantially better than only one of his seven possible hands, tied with three, and behind three, the button folded. The LHO had raised with Q♥Q♠. Because the button was paying attention to his opponents, he saved money by folding a hand that he normally would have played.

Opponents' Moods. Everyone has good days and bad days. While we urge you not to play poker on your bad days (see page 131 in Chapter 10), many of your opponents will be playing poker on these days as an escape from their troubles. Listen for signs that an opponent is having a bad day. You may hear comments about fights with a spouse or significant other, problems paying bills, troubles with taxes, issues with children, or just feeling under the weather. When a player has one of these mood swings his 'A' game vanishes; instead, he will be playing his 'C' game because his normal game has gone out the window.

A normally tight player will become loose but will usually think he's still playing tight. That means he still believes he is being conservative playing 4♣4♦ from early position and calling you down to the river. The advantage to you is that he will pay you off with hands that he should have folded.

The disadvantage is that he will occasionally give you "bad beats" when he catches cards.

When a loose player has a bad day he can either become ultra-loose or he can tighten up. If you see a normally loose opponent playing tight, he may be having a bad day. Perversely for these opponents, having a bad day may improve their game. Lucky for us, they tend to play for the action and they will revert to form when their bad day is over. However, if they are playing ultra-loose, watch out! They may turn over any two cards. Be aware of the situation and take appropriate action.

Verbal Actions. Recently, we observed a game where an early position player, who had lost all his "coin-toss" hands, had raised. The cutoff decided he could *move the early position player off of his hand* (make him lay down what could possibly be the better hand), so the cutoff re-raised with 8♦7♦. The cutoff smiled quite deliberately when he re-raised. The early position player looked at the cutoff and stated, "Well, you must have ace-king." He paused, and thought about his hand. "I've got to call. I have queens, so I call." The cutoff wasn't happy about him calling, because if the early position player had queens the cutoff needed to flop two pair, diamonds, an ace or a king in order to win the hand. The flop came A♣4♥4♠. The early position player checked, and in disgust stated, "Go ahead and bet your ace." The cutoff didn't want to disappoint him so he bet his almost-ace. The early position player folded queens face-up into the muck.

Usually, you will not be the recipient of such excellent verbal information. However, verbal cues are available *if you're listening for them!* Ignore the following at your own peril:

- Verbose players who suddenly stop talking. Why did they stop talking? Most of the time they need to consider their hand. If they were going to fold they would have nothing to consider so that means they have something.

- Quiet players who start talking. Unless the subject being discussed greatly impacts them, they are releasing nervous tension. Why? Because they've picked up a hand that makes them nervous. A hand they were going to fold isn't going to make someone nervous, so this player has something.

- A player's tone of voice changes. Usually this also indicates a release of nervous tension. Look for this player to play this hand.

When a player verbally states his hand while the hand is in progress, he may or may not be telling the truth. Most players who discuss hands do so in order to obtain information from their opponents. They will be truthful *only* when they perceive that it benefits them. Thus, you have to evaluate the motives behind the disclosure in order to determine if the information you receive is truthful.

When the example above occurred, the cutoff felt that his opponent was truthful. The early position player was unhappy in running into what he perceived was a 50-50 situation. The disgust was evident on his face. Subconsciously, the cutoff processed the information and instinctively knew that his opponent held pocket queens. Sure, the cutoff got a lucky flop, but he was able to utilize the verbal cues his opponent gave him.

Contrast this with the typical post-mortem discussion of a hand. Everyone routinely lies about what they held. Part of this is due to our subconscious not wanting to admit that we made a mistake. Say you hold A♠Q♥ and that you are raised off the hand. The eventual winner shows down his A♦J♣, while had you stayed in the hand you would have taken down a big pot. Most people will state when asked what they held that they held AT or "a smaller ace" so that they give the impression that they make a good fold. This is the correct thing to do as it causes your opponents to believe that you can correctly read when it is right to fold, thus increasing your opponent's respect for your play. Thus, don't equate post-mortem answers with actual hand holdings.

Betting Patterns. As mentioned at the beginning of this chapter, the human brain works in patterns. We recognize patterns, file by patterns, and yes, bet by patterns. Most individuals when they encounter a situation will use what last worked for them. The trick is to determine *what* they are doing.

You must follow the actions of your opponents and categorize how they bet. Do they always raise three times the big blind? Do they call with small pairs? Do they mix it up, sometimes slow-playing a big hand? There is no one answer here; you must determine how each opponent bets.

Sometimes a table will have a "standard" bring-in raise. For example, if the blinds are $1 and $2, a standard bring-in raise might be to $10. Assume this has become your table's de-facto raise. However, on this hand, a middle position player raises to $20. If his hand is shown, see if he has a medium pocket pair (a hand that many overbet the pot with in the hope that they do not get called) or some other holding. Make a note of it. If the situation recurs, you can tentatively put your opponent on a hand like the one he previously held.

Now, let's turn the situation around. If your opponents are observant, *they* will be attempting to discern *your* betting pattern. Thus, as we discuss further in Chapter 4, you should either bet the same amount whether you are on a total bluff or have AA, or your bets should be completely random. Using either method, your opponents cannot obtain a read on your betting pattern because there is none.

Reading Your Opponents

We were watching a poker event on television and one of the players made a great laydown holding the second nut flush. A friend couldn't believe he made that laydown and stated that he could never have done it. The key was going through the hand and putting together what each bet meant. Our hero held K♥T♥ in a no-limit tournament. Both players had big stacks; our hero had $500,000 while his opponent had $480,000. The blinds were $5,000 and $10,000. The table was nine-handed.

Everyone folded to our hero who made the standard raise to $35,000. After thinking for a few moments, the big blind called. The flop was Q♥9♠2♥, giving our hero the second nut flush draw and an inside straight draw. His opponent checked and our hero bet $70,000. His opponent thought for about thirty seconds and called. The pot now had $210,000 in it.

Our hero had put his opponent on middle cards, perhaps a middle pair. His opponent had committed over 20% of his chips to this hand; he must have, in some way, connected with the flop.

The turn was the 3♦, changing nothing. The opponent, after thinking for about thirty seconds, checked. Our hero also checked. The river was the 9♥ giving our hero his flush but making a full house possible. The opponent thought for about thirty seconds and bet $75,000. After thinking for about thirty seconds our hero folded.

Afterwards, our hero mentioned that once his opponent called the flop, only an inside straight or a non-pairing flush would get him to put more money into the pot. He noted that his opponent had rarely defended his blinds and then called a flop bet where the flop was quite favorable (for our hero). Our hero could not put his opponent on a hand that he could beat. For the record, the opponent held Q♦9♦ and made a full house on the river.

What our hero didn't mention was that he had played against this opponent many times and had cataloged his play. He believed that his opponent held middle cards when he called the pre-flop raise, and he *knew* that his opponent had hit the flop. He could not put his opponent on any hand he could beat on the river so he correctly folded.

Our friend felt that learning his opponents' tendencies was a daunting task. Perhaps it is, if you want to learn about *all* of your opponents immediately. Instead, we suggest you concentrate on one individual at a time. Choose someone at your table and watch everything that he does. Take surreptitious notes about the hands he plays, how he bets those hands, when he raises, when he folds, when he calls and when he checks. At the end of a typical session you'll be well on the way to knowing how he bets.

If you do this for ten sessions you'll have learned about ten of your opponents. You may also find that some of your opponents have similar characteristics. Some may be tight and bet in similar patterns. The human brain is great in finding patterns. There is a danger, though; sometimes the brain will find a pattern where there is none. For example, assume that the first three opponents you face all have red hair and are tight-aggressive players. At your next session one of your opponents has red hair. You might assume that this individual is also tight-aggressive. Just because the first three red-haired poker players you categorize are tight-aggressive, don't assume that the fourth follows the same pattern.

Types of Opponents

Your opponents will come in all shapes and varieties. No, we're not talking about their looks; rather, we are talking about their skill level. Figure 1 shows a matrix of aggression/passivity versus tightness/looseness.[9]

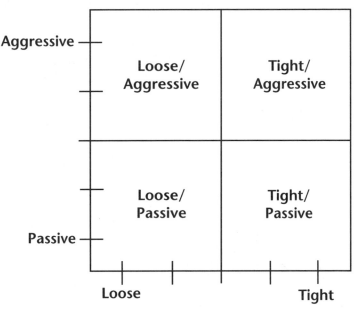

Figure 1: Player classification grid

The aggression axis measures how often a player raises. A player that never raises is very weak. A player that always comes in for a raise is very aggressive. The tightness axis measures how often a player voluntarily puts money into a pot. Everyone plays pocket Aces. Most players fold Q♦3♣

---

9. Alan Schoonmaker developed a poker "player's grid" in his *The Psychology of Poker*. Descriptive grids were first mentioned in Blake, Robert R., Jane S. Mouton, Louis B. Barnes, and Larry E. Greiner, "Breakthrough in Organization Development," *Harvard Business Review*, November-December 1964 and Blake, Robert R. and Jane S. Mouton, *The Managerial Grid*, Houston: Gulf Publishing, 1964.

from early position. The more hands a player plays, the looser he is. These are the different types of players you're likely to find (based on this scale).

The Tight-Passive Player. This player plays few hands and rarely raises. When he has the nuts on the river, he will bet and/or raise. When this player does bet (or raise), look out! He has a monster. You can usually raise this player out of pots. He's in over his head when playing no-limit hold'em.

The Loose-Passive Player. This player plays a lot of hands, but rarely bets or raises. He is the prototypical "calling station"—a player you *cannot* usually raise out of a pot. This player loses money in all forms of poker, especially no-limit.

The Loose-Aggressive Player. This player will play almost any two cards, usually for a raise. He's the maniac of the table. When you have one maniac in a game, you need to tighten up and let the maniac bet for you. Usually, you will be dividing up his money with a few other players. A game with multiple maniacs can be a frightening spectacle: a very high variance game for good players but one where the maniacs are right at home. There are a few maniacs who can successfully utilize this type of play (they are excellent flop players and have superior reading skills). However, in small buy-in no-limit hold'em, the maniac strategy rarely succeeds.

The Tight-Aggressive Player. She doesn't play many hands. Typically, she comes in for a raise. She's not afraid to bet "on the come" (when she's drawing) if she has the right odds. Everyone thinks she's lucky. If you're in a game where everyone else is tight-aggressive, leave the game. You'll need good cards and luck to win any money here, and there are better games to be found.

The Internet-Style Player. When you play no-limit hold'em online (on the Internet), it's easy to just click the "raise" button. Most online sites make the default raise one big bet (i.e., with $1 and $2 blinds, the raise will be to $4). If one of your opponents tends to just double the bet, most likely he's been reared on Internet poker. (In Chapter 4 we discuss why just doubling the bet is poor strategy.) Additionally, most Internet-style players are aggressive because it is much easier to "click" on a button to bet than to physically toss chips into a pot.

So what type of player are you? Are you tight-passive or loose-passive? Don't give up hope! In the coming chapters we will show you a strategy for no-limit hold'em that should move you towards being a dangerous foe at the tables. For now, recognize that your opponents are of *all* types and that you need to categorize them while at the table.

Hopefully, this chapter has given you a flavor for the kinds of opponents you will face when playing no-limit hold'em. Most new players believe that reading your opponents is a skill you either inherit or you don't (like red hair). On the contrary, for most players, reading opponents is a learned skill. If you keep practicing, you *will* improve.

Chapter 4
Play Topics I: Odds and Betting Strategies

N o-limit hold'em is a complex game. There are far more factors to consider before acting in no-limit than there are in limit. At times, the task of keeping all of these things in perspective can be daunting. One of these topics is the concept and application of odds. We're about to discuss pot odds and how they affect your decision making at the table, but before we begin, we want to emphasize that understanding pot odds is not a difficult task at all. In fact, with a few simple examples, you will be surprised at how easy this topic is to grasp. Once a few basic concepts are presented, you will begin to clearly understand the math behind poker and why certain hands are played in different ways depending upon the situation.

Another topic that might have confused you in the past is betting strategies. How much should you bet in a given situation? How much is too much or too little? What do certain bets mean? Again, once you begin to understand the basic math behind poker, you will see why it is sometimes correct to make a bet larger than you might expect, or smaller in some cases. Remember this: *no-limit hold'em is not played like limit hold'em*.

With a basic comprehension of the following two topics, you will be much better prepared for battle. We recommend you read this chapter several times before going on to the next chapter. It is essential that you grasp these concepts, as we will be referring to them later in the book.

Pot Odds

Simply stated, *pot odds* is the price the pot is laying you to make a call. For example, if there is $40 in the pot and it will cost you $10 to call, the pot is laying you $40 to $10, more commonly simplified as 4 to 1. Similarly, if there is $120 in the pot and the price to call is $60, you are getting 2 to 1 on your call. If the pot is $300 and it is $5 to call (a very rare situation), you are getting 60 to 1.

That's all there is to it. Now, how does this help you in your decision making? Ah, now we come to the important part. Let's say you are holding A♦Q♦ in late position. The blinds are $2 and $3, and after three limpers, you decide to raise to $12. Everyone, including the big blind, calls your raise. Five players see the flop with $60 in the pot (5 x $12 = $60, we'll ignore the rake in this example for simplicity). The flop comes J♦6♦3♣. The first player bets $20, the next player folds while the last two limpers call. Should you call?

The first thing you will need to know is the odds of you making your hand (assuming it will be the best hand). When you flop four to a flush, the odds against you making your flush on the turn are approximately 4.2 to 1. We'll round that to 4 to 1 for this example. So, you are going to need at least 4 to 1 odds from the pot to call a bet. After the early position player bet $20, there was $80 in the pot. Once the other two limpers called, there is now $120 in the pot. It costs you $20 to call, so the pot is laying you $120 to $20, or 6 to 1. It is an easy call.[10]

OK, so you have called the bet on the flop. There is now $140 in the pot. The turn brings the 9♥. Not the card you were looking for, but you still have the best draw and two *overcards* (cards higher than any card on the board). The

---

10. Raising is also a valid move in this spot, but we'll discuss that later.

early position bettor now bets $80. This time, both limpers fold. What do you do?

After the bet, there is now $220 in the pot. With one card to come, you are a 4.1 to 1 underdog to make your flush on the river. It's going to cost you $80 to call, so the pot is laying you odds of $220 to $80, or approximately 2.75 to 1. Even if we attempted to factor in the value of your overcards rivering the best pair, you do not have the odds to call this bet, so you fold.

Calculating the odds to make your hand on the next card is fairly simple. Let's take the example of a straight draw. Say you have limped in late position with 8♣7♣. The flop comes 9♠6♥A♣, giving you an open-ended straight draw (any 10 or 5 gives you a straight). What are your odds of making your straight on the next card?

You already know five of the 52 cards in the deck, so there are 47 unknown cards remaining. Of those 47 cards, eight will make your hand (four 5s and four 10s). So, there are 39 bad cards and 8 good cards. Dividing the 39 by 8, we see that your odds of making your straight on the turn are 4.9 to 1.

Implied Odds

If you have been playing poker for any length of time, you have probably heard someone justify a call by claiming he had implied odds to call. Often this is just an excuse for making a loose call, but not always. So what are implied odds?

Let's go back to a previous example. You raised with A♦Q♦, only this time you are in early middle position instead of late position. The same four players have seen the flop for $12 each (including yourself) and on the flop there is $60. The flop again comes J♦6♦3♣, and the early position player bets $20 as before. However, in this example, you have to act before the other three players. There is $80 in the pot, and it is going to cost you $20 to call, meaning that you are getting odds of 4 to 1. As we know, the odds of making your flush on the turn are 4.2 to 1, so you are not quite getting enough odds to make the call. But before you fold that hand, take a moment. What about the three players behind you? Assume they have been passive, and usually call most bets on the flop and even the turn. What if you fold, but two of them call the $20 bet after you fold? You will wish you had called the bet, because then you would be getting that same 6 to 1 on your call. Your immediate call gives you 4 to 1 odds, but your implied odds are (with two callers after you) 6 to 1. This means that instead of folding you should call. Anticipated future money in the pot is the basis for implied odds.

Let's take another example. Suppose you are faced with a bet on the turn with the nut flush draw. The pot is only laying you 3.5 to 1 on your call. However, you believe that if you make your hand, you will be able to make a very large amount of money on the river by trapping the loose bettor for most of his stack. This future money gives you great implied odds, so you call the bet.

The theory of *implied odds* simply states that you need to sometimes take future bets into consideration when you are making a call (or raise). Sometimes these future bets can be enough to turn a fold into a call. However, implied odds also work in the opposite direction.

Continuing with our flush example, you see that there are three players yet to act after you, and although you are not getting the proper pot odds to make the call on the flop, you believe that at least two of the loose/passive players behind you will call if you call, so you toss in your $20. But surprise of surprises, the next player now raises to $100. Now it is going to cost you another $80 to continue with the hand. If the last two players plus the original bettor now fold, the pot lays you $200 to $80, or 5 to 2. This is not nearly enough to call to chase your flush, so you fold. The concept of future raises such as this is called *reverse implied odds*. Reverse implied odds come into play when it is most likely going to cost you more to chase your draws than might be apparent. In this example, instead of costing you only $20 to see the turn, it costs $100, and had you anticipated that the pot would be raised, you most likely wouldn't (and shouldn't) have called the bet. To further complicate the matter, what if you decide to foolishly call this bet, only to have one of the loose limpers behind you re-raise all-in? The reverse implied odds are now grossly working against you.

To avoid adverse situations like this you must know your players. In some situations with passive players, you may be getting good implied odds to call a bet; however, if the players yet to act are aggressive, it might be best to fold. As we discussed in Chapter 3, knowing the tendencies of your opponents is a key element. And when it comes to implied odds or reverse implied odds, making correct assessments of your opponents is crucial.

Before we leave this section, let's look at a few more examples of odds. This topic is very important, and the concepts here will often be the determining factor in some of your close decisions at the table.

Example 1: You are in the small blind holding K♥9♦. This is not, in most cases, a playable hand. We'll again assume that the blinds are $2 and $3. There are seven limpers to you. Do you call or fold this trash hand? With the big blind plus seven limpers, there is now $26 in the pot (your $2 small blind, plus $21 from the seven limpers, plus $3 from the big blind). It is going to cost you $1 to call, so you are getting 26 to 1 on your call. It's a simple decision. In fact, this example is one of common occurrence. When you are getting odds this good in the small blind, there are very few hands you can fold. There are arguments for folding some of your very worst hands such as 72o, 93o etc., but for the most part, you will throw in the extra chip and see a flop. What you are looking for is a monster flop. Implied odds—as well as the current pot odds—are key determinants of this strategy. If the flop comes very favorable to you, your $1 investment was well worth it.

The key to this situation is your ability to fold, even if the flop seems to hit you pretty good. For example, if you hold 9♥7♦ in the small blind and the flop comes A♠7♠7♣, you could be in big trouble. Most likely, you will call on the flop. However, if there is adverse betting, a fold is indicated. In any case, unless the turn is favorable, you shouldn't continue betting with the hand.

Example 2: In late position, you have limped with J♥T♥ after several limpers. No one raises, and you see the flop six-handed. The flop is Q♥7♥4♠. There is $18 in the pot. The first player bets $10. It is a loose game, and 3 players call the bet before it gets back to you. There is $58 in the pot and it's going to cost you $10 to call. The pot is offering you 5.8 to 1. You are roughly 4 to 1 to make your flush, and you figure it to be the best hand if it hits; thus, your implied odds are even higher. As well as the flush, you have several different *back-door* (you need two running cards) straight draws. These don't add a lot of value, especially in a no-limit game where the bets are sure to escalate, but they must also be considered. You have an easy call.

Example 3: It is the same situation as above, but this time only one player calls the bet on the flop. With $18 in the pot pre-flop, there is now $38 in the pot. It is $10 to call, so you are now getting 3.8 to 1 on your call. Although the implied odds might warrant a call, it is still a very close decision, and you may want to fold here and wait for a better situation.

Example 4: Continuing with the example above, let's now move your seat to middle/early position. Now, instead of limping with your J♥T♥, you have raised to $12. As is typical in these loose games, three players have cold-called your raise, as well as the early limper. Both blinds have folded. You see the flop five-handed. There is $65 in the pot (5 players at $12 each, plus $5 in blinds). The flop is the same Q♥7♥4♠ as above. The first player bets only $10, giving you 7.5 to 1 on your call. However, a quick look to your left gives you some great information; a late position player has casually grabbed three green $25 chips. You are pretty sure he's going to make a raise, and if you call for $10 here, you might be facing a much larger amount when it comes back to you. Your odds aren't nearly what they might seem to be now, as reverse implied odds have now come into play. As you can see, this is an interesting hand to use as an example as several different odds concepts come up.

Let's say that there was nothing to your left indicating a large raise. You are truly getting 7.5 to 1 on your call. Do you call? The answer, as it does in so many poker situations, depends on many factors. Are the players behind you likely to raise? If so, reverse implied odds might prevent you from calling. Are your opponents calling stations, willing to call even if you raise here? If so, you might be getting correct odds to raise (pot odds aren't used only when deciding to call or fold).

And what if the player in front of you bets $30? Now the pot is offering you $95 to $30, or about 3.2 to 1. You'd like better odds for your flush, so you decide to fold—but wait a minute! What about the players left to act behind you? Remember implied odds? If you knew that at least one of them was going to call the $30 bet, you'd have correct odds to call because your odds are now at least 4.2 to 1.

Pot odds, implied odds and reverse implied odds play a big part in most decisions you will make when involved in a hand. As we have seen, they are not only used for drawing situations, but also for raising situations. Proper odds can help you determine whether or not you can call. Implied odds help you in determining future bets you might earn if you make your hand, and reverse implied odds help you to determine just how much more you might have to invest into a pot after your initial call. All of these concepts will be useful to you during your poker career. Learn them now, and they will become intuitive in the future.

Betting Strategies

Unlike limit poker, no-limit allows the player to bet any amount he desires—as long as it is at least equal to the big blind, or to the last bet (or raise) in that round. For example, if the blinds are $2 and $3, the smallest allowed pre-flop raise would be $3. A player making it "$6 to go" has made the minimum pre-flop raise. On the flop, if a player has bet $14, the smallest raise would be to $28 (a raise of $14). In this case, a player can bet any amount from $14 to his whole stack. Indeed, you can *always* bet your entire stack at any time.[11]

With the above in mind, how do you decide the proper amount to bet? That's an excellent question. One of the biggest mistakes we see in the small no-limit games of today is improper betting. Players tend to bet and raise amounts that are far too small in these games, probably because they are used to playing limit poker. However, some players take the concept to the other extreme and tend to move all-in way too of-

---

11. There is one exception to betting your whole stack. Assume that you have bet $10, and a player goes all-in for $12. Another player calls the $12. In most games, you will *not* be allowed to re-raise in this situation because the all-in players' raise is *not* a full raise. (Depending on the casino, the all-in raise must either be a full raise, $10 in this case, or half of a full raise, $5 in this case. The $2 all-in raise is neither.) Your only options in this situation are to call the $2 raise or to fold.

ten. While there is no magic formula for determining proper betting strategies, we do have some guidelines to offer. We will also point out some of the major mistakes players frequently make in betting and explain why these are usually errors.

Pre-flop Betting

Before the flop, the only options available are call, raise or fold. There is no "betting." You can call the amount of the big blind, raise, or release your hand and wait for the next. If you call, the amount is already determined for you, but what if you find yourself in a situation where you'd like to raise? How much do you raise?

One of the most common raising mistakes you will see in today's small no-limit games is a raise to two times the big blind. This is the minimum raise one can make. This raise has become popular, we believe, because of the huge popularity of online poker. At most online poker rooms, there is a *slider* control that allows you to determine the amount of your raise, but there is also a raise button. This button automatically doubles the last bet or raise. Pre-flop, this raise button will make a raise to two times the size of the big blind. For example, if the blinds are $1 and $2, hitting the raise button will make it $4 to go. This small raise is usually incorrect (we'll explain why in a moment). Further, it is not uncommon to see a player re-raise or even four-bet the minimum pre-flop. These players are playing the game as if it is limit, and in doing so, they're giving up a huge advantage.

The *two-times raise* (double the amount of the previous bet or raise) described above is usually incorrect because it accomplishes neither of the two main objectives of raising. A pre-flop raise is designed to either limit the field or to build the pot. This minimum raise usually scares no one, and those players who had planned to limp will most likely still do so. As for building the pot, doubling the big blind is a poor way to get the job done. If there are four players in the hand, the pot before the flop is now $16 instead of $8. It *is* a doubling of the pot, but the same could be accomplished with a larger raise, and this raise also would have established you as the aggressor. A small minimum raise doesn't show much strength. Don't be surprised at the number of players who will still call a legitimate raise, such as four times the size of the big blind. If you had made the above raise to $8 and only two players had called, the pot would be $24. You have accomplished a narrowing of the field and a larger pot.

On the other end of the spectrum, many players will raise to a far too high dollar amount before the flop. For example, in our example with $1 and $2 blinds, it is not uncommon to see someone bring it in for $20 or even more. Some players will even move all-in pre-flop to win the blinds. This is maniacal. Raising such a large amount to win $3 to $5 in blinds is suicide. In most cases, you are only going to get a call from a player who has you beat. Let us repeat this because it's so important. *If you move all-in to win the blinds, you will only get called by a very powerful hand or by an occasional maniac.* Sure, you would like to get called if you are holding aces, but the chances are that no one will call you. Yet we see this mistake all the time. Apparently, the glamour of poker on television has caused players to think that the best move is to move all of your chips in at any time to win the pot. There is a lot more to winning no-limit hold'em than just moving in.

So what is the proper raise pre-flop? As we stated earlier, there are no hard and fast rules. The technique we advise here is solid, but is only meant as a guideline. There will be times you will want to deviate from this strategy, and there will even be times when you will want to make the minimum raise or even move it all-in pre-flop. Those times are rare, but they do occur. In general, however, if you follow this sim-ple guide, you will usually be making the correct raise.

If you are the first one to enter the pot after the blinds, make a raise equal to four times the big blind. For example, you are in early position holding A♥K♥. If the blinds are $1 and $2, make it $8 to go. This is a standard raise. Often, players will use the phrase "three to five times the big blind" as their opening raise. We'll split the difference and use four. It is up to you. As another example, if the blinds are $2 and $3, your standard opening raise would be to $12.

But what if you are not the first one in the pot? No problem. To thin the field or to build the pot, just add one additional big blind to your raise for each player who has limped in. Here are some examples:

Example 1: The blinds are $1 and $2. Three players have limped and you hold J♦J♠. Make the raise to $14 (4 x $2 + $2 for each of the three limpers).

Example 2: The blinds are $1 and $2. Six players have called the big blind. You hold 9♠9♣ and decide to raise. Make it $20 to go (4 x $2 plus $2 for each of the six limpers).

Example3: The blinds are $2 and $3. Four players have limped in and you look down to find A♣Q♣. Make it $24.

In each of these cases, your raise will either narrow the field or increase the size of the pot. In no-limit hold'em, your usu-al goal is to increase the size of the pot while giving you the *aggression initiative*. By this, we mean that you become the aggressor in the hand, and players still in the hand on the flop and beyond will almost always *check to the raiser* on the flop (although this is often incorrect), and now you have the edge. If you have narrowed the field, you have few-er hands to worry about drawing out on you or calling your bet on the flop if you have missed. If you have simply built a big pot, it allows you to make a rather large bet on the flop, thus chasing out possible better hands that might ordinarily call a smaller bet.

We mentioned earlier that there are some occasions where you want to make the minimum raise. One of these occasions is when you are looking to induce a re-raise. For example, you are holding AA and there is a very aggressive player in the game who loves to re-raise before the flop. You might make the minimum raise, and then move-in on him (or at least make a very large re-raise, depending on how deep both stacks are) when he re-raises your tiny raise.

Less common is the occasion to move all-in before the flop when no one has yet raised. This play is usually made out of the blinds to win a large amount of blind/limp money already in the pot. For example, you are in the small blind with A♦9♦. *Everyone* has called the big blind of $3. You can usually make a very large raise (sometimes all-in) and pick up the pot without a flop. If you don't mind being faced with the occasional call (sometimes by a big hand that limped, but usually by marginal hands like A♣J♠ or worse), this play can be very effective. However, try not to overuse it.

A second situation to use this play is one or two orbits after you have done it with a hand like A♦9♦ *except* that now you hold a legitimate big hand, such as K♦K♣. If you are up against players who believe you are stealing, this all-in move is quite effective. However, it must be done while it is very fresh in your opponents' memories that you will raise all-in with marginal hands.

So far, we have covered the pre-flop raise. But what about the re-raise? Sometimes you will be dealt a powerhouse hand like AA or KK and you will want to re-raise a pre-flop raiser. You most likely have the best hand, and it is best to get your money in when you are a favorite. You will also usually have one or two very loose raisers in your game, and re-raising can be a valuable tool to slow them down or make them pay for their loose standards.

In general, your pre-flop re-raise should be between $2\,{}^1\!/_2$ and 3 times the size of the pre-flop raise. So, if the pre-flop raiser has made it $8 to go, your re-raise might be to $20 or $25.[12] Again, it is important to not just double the original raise. If he has enough of a hand to raise, he will usually call your re-raise, so make it worthwhile. Here are some examples:

Example 1: The pre-flop raiser has raised the $3 big blind to only $6. You have QQ and decide to re-raise to $18. As noted, for simplicity, you can just make the raise to $20.

Example 2: A loose, aggressive player has made it $15 to go. You should re-raise to between $40 and $50.

If the pre-flop raise has already been cold-called by one or more players, you will need to increase the size of your re-raise. A practical rule might be to add the size of the raise for each cold-caller. For example, the $3 big blind has been raised to $10 and two players have cold-called. You might want to make it $50 to go.

Depending on your stack sizes, there are times when you will want to just re-raise all-in. For example, if the game has a $100 maximum buy-in, and all the stacks are fairly close (perhaps the game has just started), it may be correct to re-raise all-in, especially if one or more players have already cold-called the pre-flop raise.

If you are re-raised pre-flop, you need to make a decision. Do you simply call the re-raise, do you make another re-raise, or do you fold? In general, just calling the re-raise is a weak play. It is showing weakness to your opponent who

---

12. $25 is more than three times $8, but often your raise or re-raise will be in common amounts, rounded up or down from the guidelines. In this case, we took a 3x re-raise and rounded up $1.

will almost always come out betting into you on the flop. If you have been fortunate enough to flop a monster, this is no problem. But if you have flopped top pair or even a slightly better hand, you don't know where you are. Playing the hand from this position is extremely difficult.

With your marginal raising hands, you should probably fold. This is not showing weakness in most games, although in some very aggressive games, you might be giving up a small edge. This is showing that you will raise with a variety of hands, and sometimes you will not have a hand worth playing to a re-raise. It will make you much harder to read on the flop and beyond.

With your strongest hands, you will want to re-raise. This includes AA-KK, and possibly QQ. We say possibly with QQ because this is a hand you might want to call with and see a flop. The re-raiser might have AK, and on a little flop, you will often have the best hand. A lot depends on the raiser. Is he loose and aggressive? If so, you can play more hands against his re-raise. If he is passive or tight, you might want to think twice about playing anything worse than kings against him.

This leads us to an interesting situation. What if you believe you are being bullied by an aggressive player? Do you fight back with your marginal hand? You can do this *only* if you have a fairly strong read on your opponent. If he's the type of player to raise or re-raise just to push around his opponents, you will eventually have to put him to the test and send in the big guns (by moving all-in). Even if you don't have a hand, there will come a time when you need to make a stand against these overly aggressive players. You can't let them pick at your stack all night long. They will bleed you dry over time if you let them. Put them to a decision for all of their chips once or twice, and you will earn respect—not only from the raiser, but from the rest of the table as well. And once you establish power and dominance at the table, your options become many. No-limit hold'em is a power struggle, and those with the power are usually the ones who go home with the money. Playing like a wimp is not a good strategy. If these aggressive actions are too much for you, you may want to stick to limit poker.

One last topic we will cover in pre-flop betting strategies is the limp/re-raise play. The opportunity for this play usually exists when there is a constant raiser in the game. If you are dealt a monster hand, AA-QQ, you can often just limp in anticipation of a raise from the loose maniac, and when it gets back to you, you can trap those who have already called the loose player's raise by making a large re-raise. This play can also be made when you are holding a marginal hand, or no hand at all, when you think a limp/re-raise will win you the pot without seeing a flop. A lot depends on the callers of the original raise, and even the raiser himself. If he is a loose raiser that will often fold to heavy pressure, go for it. However, if he is a loose caller as well as a loose raiser, only limp/re-raise with your better hands. And beware of this play being made against you. A limp/re-raise almost always means aces (sometimes kings), and if this play is made by a tight player, you are likely in trouble.

Betting Strategies on the Flop and Beyond

Just as you will often see the smallest allowable pre-flop raises (the size of the big blind), as well as the smallest allowable re-raises (the size of the last raise), you will see this practice continued on the flop and other betting rounds. Often, you will see a player cold-call a pre-flop raise and then bet the minimum on the flop into a raised pot with several opponents. You will also see a player raise pre-flop only to bet the minimum on the flop and all rounds after.

Apparently, many players are having difficulty making the adjustment from limit hold'em to no-limit. One of the reasons for this, as explained earlier in this chapter, is the advent of Internet poker and the ever-present bet/raise button. This button will always make the minimum bet or raise. This betting strategy, while almost always incorrect, brings up an interesting dilemma. When faced with a player who constantly bets and raises (or even re-raises) the minimum allowable amount, how do you put that player on a hand? In no-limit, hand reading skills involve a study of the betting patterns of your opponents. When a player will raise the minimum whether he is holding AA or K♠9♠, and then bet the minimum on the flop, how can you determine his hand?

The answer, of course, is a matter of knowing your opponents, their tendencies, and even where they do most of their playing. If one of your opponents learned poker from playing online, he'll be more apt to make this kind of play. If you find one of your opponents constantly moving all-in, it is a good bet that he has seen a great deal of poker on television. Players emulate what they see, and if one of their heroes re-raises all-in with what is essentially an unplayable hand, they believe it is the proper move.[13]

If you have raised pre-flop, it is usually correct to bet the flop. We'll cover this more in Chapter 7, but for now, keep in mind that aggression before the flop usually requires aggression on the flop, regardless of your hand. This is not always the case, as you will see, but even if you miss the flop entirely, a strong bet on the flop often will win the pot with surprising regularity.

There are no hard and fast rules as to how much you should bet. It all depends upon what you want to accomplish. As

---

13. Of course, what these students of the game don't realize is that the expert players making moves like this are playing the player, not the cards. When Gus Hansen cold-calls a pre-flop raise with 9♥6♥, he's not doing it because he values the quality of the cards. More often than not, plays like this are to set up future plays based upon current observation.

mentioned earlier, it is often the case that you will intentionally underbet or overbet the pot to achieve a certain result. We'll go into those particular plays in a moment. For now, let's take a look at "normal" betting.

The normal bet on the flop is somewhere between half the size of the pot and the size of the pot. For example, you raised pre-flop in a $2/$3 blind game to $12 and three players called. With four players paying $12, there is $48 in the pot on the flop (less the rake). A normal bet would be between $25 and $50, and the most likely bet would be about $40.

Another example might be a loose-passive game where seven players have limped for $3 each, and on the flop, the pot is $21. A standard bet here would be about $15. If there are three callers here on the flop, the pot on the turn would be $66, and a normal bet would be between $45 and $65. Again, we want to stress that these are not hard and fast rules. It is important to realize that every player will have their own strategy and playing style, and what might be considered a normal bet by some might be too small or too large for others, and they will change their style accordingly. Only keen observation will help you determine what each bet means.

Betting in hold'em tends to escalate in the later rounds. In a limit game, the turn and river bets are usually double the pre-flop and flop bets. In no-limit, the betting also increases, but it is usually in relation to the size of the pot. Quite often, river bets are exponentially larger than pre-flop raises, and it is not uncommon to see one or even several players all-in when the last card is turned. This is the nature of no-limit, and it is why so much is made or lost in a single session. At any given time, your whole stack is at stake. It is imperative that you maintain proper mental control and avoid any impulsive actions while betting. If you make an impulsive bet or raise in limit, you may lose one or two bets. An impulsive bet or raise in no-limit could mean a trip to the ATM.

Overbetting the pot is something you might want to do on occasion. Overbetting simply means betting more than the size of the pot. Beginning players typically overbet the pot when they do not want a call. For example, a player who limped in with A♥8♦ might overbet the pot on the flop if it comes ace-high. The kicker isn't strong, and if a player calls or plays back, he'll usually have to slow down on the turn or simply fold.

With this in mind, you can sometimes overbet the pot against an observant player when you want a call. This is most effective when you have the table image of a poor player. Your more astute opponents may believe that you don't want to be called, and they'll raise you. If you are playing against this kind of player, an overbet may be the correct play to extract the most chips on your big hand. After you receive a call, you can check on the turn (to look weak) and then make a large raise when your opponent bets. If you overbet the flop and your opponent raises, you can usually make your move without seeing the turn.

Don't take the concept of overbetting too far, however. Top players will recognize this and you might lose some bets you would have otherwise picked up had you bet a more reasonable amount.

Underbetting the pot is generally a play made by players with a decent hand but not a great hand. They feel that, if they bet a little, they can usually find out where they are in the hand, and if that raise comes, escape from the hand will be inexpensive. The problem with underbetting (often this underbet is the minimum allowed) is that it will often give opponents a correct price to chase draws. Remember our discussion of pot odds? If the pot is $40 on the flop and your opponent bets $5, you are getting 9 to 1 on your call, and a flush draw is now profitable. Had your opponent bet $30, you'd be getting only 7 to 3, which isn't enough to justify a call.

How many times have you witnessed a player *flat betting* (betting the same amount on all betting rounds) through the river, and then lament his bad luck when an opponent caught the right card to make a flush? Was this bad luck? No, because he wasn't betting enough. *This may be the single biggest mistake (aside from hand selection) in no-limit hold'em.* Betting too small can be death in this game. When you lay your opponents proper odds to chase by not protecting your hand, you will often find yourself on the losing end of a hand you should have easily won. It is fine to slow-play a monster hand, but with most of your top pair or two pair hands, you will want to apply the pressure with bets and raises.

There is a situation when you might want to underbet the pot. If you find yourself in a game with a very aggressive player, and you have a big hand, you might want to bet very small (even the minimum) if you anticipate a raise. This will allow you to re-raise and, often, the aggressive player will let his ego take control and you can take his whole stack. Further, this will also allow you to trap the less-observant players at your table, and when you re-raise, they will be forced to fold or to call with weak holdings. Either way, it is good for you. This play shouldn't be used very often, as you have to be sure you will be raised, but against the right type of player in the right situation, it can be deadly for your ego-driven opponent.

Betting in no-limit hold'em takes experience. Over time, you will gain a feel for the game and for the individual opponents you will be facing. You will learn what works against them and what does not. If you are used to playing limit poker, this adjustment might be difficult and awkward at first, but experience will help you develop a betting style that is your own and that you will feel comfortable with. If you think before each bet, and determine what your objectives are, your bets will usually be correct.

Chapter 5
Position

Introduction to the Matrix Theory of No-Limit Hold'em

I n many poker books you see a listing of hands that you can play based on position. While a good hand selection chart is a nice guideline, the game of no-limit hold'em requires a bit more. Enter the Matrix Theory. Simply stated, the Matrix Theory combines not only the starting hands you'll be playing, but other determining factors as well. What is your position? What is your relative position (to the button or to certain players) and what has occurred before you act? What might occur after you act? What is your stack size and what are the stack sizes of your opponents? What type of opponents are you facing? All of these factors combine in a matrix, and it is from this matrix that we can begin to understand what hands to play and how to play them.

Position is, by far, the most important factor in determining the hands you play. However, as mentioned above, in no-limit hold'em there are other factors besides position that need to be considered in order to determine whether you play a hand.

Let's look at a hand from a $5/$10 *limit* hold'em game. You are in a middle position and are dealt 8♠8♥. An early position player raises and the player to your right calls. You elect to call, as it is only $10 with the chance of winning at least $27. Yes, someone in late position may raise but you are fairly certain you will have the right price.

Now let's assume you are dealt the same hand, 8♠8♥, in a $1/$2 blind $100 buy-in no-limit hold'em game. Again, an early position player raises. However, the raiser doesn't just double the big blind; rather, he makes it $12. Again, the player to your right calls. What do you do with your pair of eights?

Frankly, we have not given you enough information to decide. Other vital information you must know before deciding your action includes:

- Relative stack sizes of you and your opponents
- Your image (and that of your opponents)
- The types of opponents you face (see Chapter 3)
- Skill levels of yourself and your opponents

Position

Most successful poker players quickly learn about the value of being in late position: it is much easier to win a hand when you have fewer opponents. Actually, there are two types of position: physical and relative. *Physical position* refers to your position relative to the button. If you are first or second to act pre-flop, we consider you to be in early position. If you are on the button or just to the right of the button (the cut-off position), you are in late position. If you are not in early or late position (or in one of the blinds), you are in middle position. The blinds are a special case, as they act last pre-flop, but must act first after the flop.

The later your physical position, the more hands you can play pre-flop. Most players in early position will throw a trouble hand such as K♥J♣ into the muck. However, this hand may be worth a raise from late position if you are the first player (other than the blinds) to enter the pot.

After the flop, your *relative position* becomes extremely important. This concept simply describes when you act in comparison to your remaining opponents. Suppose you raise from middle position and your only caller is one of the blinds. You now act last on each round of betting and have the best relative position. (This is sometimes referred to as "buying the button,"[14] as you are effectively in the same position the button enjoys: last to act.)

Your Cards

If you are dealt 7♣2♥, your position is not that important: you have the ultimate in trash hands and should muck from any position in almost any situation. There are 169 possible starting hands in hold'em (ignoring suits). Most of these starting hands should rarely be played.

You may see poker—especially no-limit hold'em—described as a people game played with cards. While this is true, and the nature of your opponents is vital (see below), today's games are filled with players who have no concept of hand values, stack size, position, and other important concepts. They have "learned" how to play no-limit hold'em by watching the final tables of the *World Poker Tour* and the *World Series of Poker*. Short-handed play at a final table of a tournament differs tremendously from small cash game no-limit hold'em, yet we continually see players raising (and even worse, calling) with hands like T♠6♣ regardless of position.

The late Woody Hayes said of the forward pass, "Three things can happen when you throw a forward pass, and two of them are bad." Similarly, when you bet or raise, three

---

14. "Buying the button" can also refer to a player posting both blinds from what would normally be the small blind position. Assume that a player has missed his big blind. The dealer puts an "out" button in front of his chips, and the player to his left posts the big blind. The missing player then returns; some casinos allow for "buying the button." In this scenario, the player posts both blinds. On the following hand, he gets the button and his left-hand opponent, who had the big blind when the player missed his big blind, now posts the small blind.

things can happen and two of them are good: you can win the pot right there or you can win the pot at the showdown. Because many of your opponents have no idea about card strength and will call you with almost anything, you must consider the strength of your hand when deciding whether or not to bet or raise.

The Rule of 13

One of the authors was sitting in a no-limit hold'em game and was dealt a series of trash hands such as K♦3♣, 9♥4♠, 8♣5♦, T♦3♠, and 9♠4♥. After folding 23 hands in a row, one of the other players asked if he would ever play a hand. The author responded that the Rule of 13 prevented him from playing any of these hands. While the remark was made in jest, there is some logic behind the rule.

The Rule of 13 says to add the blackjack value of your two cards (all ten-value cards are worth ten and aces are worth one). If they sum to 13, fold. The rule is a mnemonic designed to reinforce the idea that you should not play trash hands. If you fold your trash hands without thinking, you will be a step above many of your opponents. (In certain situations in late position, 76 is playable. This hand, though, is the only playable hand that adds to 13 and, more often than not, it too should be folded.)

Relative Stack Sizes

Many of today's no-limit hold'em cash games have fixed buy-ins of $100 or $200. In order to obtain a large stack size you must win the chips. This has a major impact on strategy while playing no-limit hold'em.

In a game where you can buy in for any amount (such as the $100 minimum buy-in game with $1/$2 blinds at Binion's Horseshoe), you can execute a bullying strategy by buying-in for more than anyone else at the table. Suppose that everyone else at the table has between $100 and $600 at the table and you buy-in for $2000. You can play a loose-aggressive style and make life very difficult for your opponents. Contrast that game with a new $100 fixed buy-in game. In this game stack size on the first hand is irrelevant: everyone will have $100 in front of them.

One of the authors recently sat in a $100 fixed buy-in no-limit hold'em game that had run all night. The other eight players all had stacks of at least $800 apiece. The table's de-facto bring in raise (the blinds were $2/$3) was $50! Needless to say, the strategy for that particular situation was quite different than for a new fixed buy-in game.

Stack size impacts how players play hands. Some of your opponents will tighten up when they have won a lot of money because they do not want to risk their winnings. Other people will loosen up when they have a large stack as they consider their winnings "free money." Players with a small stack may be forced to move all-in, as that may be their only reasonable bet. You ignore your opponents' stack sizes at your own peril.

Image

Assume you are sitting in a loose $100 buy-in $1/$2 blinds no-limit hold'em game. You have (rightly) folded your last 27 hands (you were dealt 7♥2♣ each hand!). On the next hand you are one to the right of the button and look down at K♣9♣. Everyone folds to you. While this hand is definitely not a premium hand, you decide to raise. Your opponents are likely to put you on a premium hand because this is the first hand you have played in some time. This is an example of using your image.

The loose player can also use his image. Assume an opponent has been consistently raising one in every three hands. Does he have a premium hand each time? It is almost impossible for him to be that lucky! More likely, he has been bullying the table. However, the loose player will also raise when he gets a premium hand, and he will likely win a larger pot than other players because his opponents are not likely to believe that the loose player actually has good cards.

Over an infinite amount of time everyone holds the same cards. Unfortunately, none of us live to experience an infinite number of hands. Some days the deck will run you over while other days you struggle with mediocre holding following mediocre holding. Tight players who judiciously raise use their image to their benefit.

Skill

Every player you encounter will have a different skill set. Some of your opponents may be experts while others are just starting to play poker. Some may have played thousands of hands of no-limit hold'em while others have played primarily limit hold'em and do not understand the differences between the games.

When we sit down in a no-limit hold'em game, we observe the other players to determine if they have any exploitable weaknesses. For example, limit hold'em players often call bets in no-limit hold'em when they do not have the correct pot odds. Additionally, we note the players' tendencies. Some of this relates to physical and verbal tells as described in Chapter 3. But we're also categorizing players as to their skills:

- Are they deceptive?
- Are they aggressive?

- Do they like to slow-play?
- Do they like to come from behind or lead in the betting?
- Are they nervous?
- Do they play too many hands?
- Can they read other players' hands?

Overall, the question we're asking is: are they skillful players or not? David Sklansky noted in his "Fundamental Theorem of Poker" that when you play a hand differently than you would have if you could see all of the cards, your opponents gain; conversely, every time your opponents play a hand differently than they would if they could see all of the cards, they lose.[15] You want to play against opponents who make mistakes. If you sit down at a table against players who play perfectly, you are going to have a tough time winning money.

Looking at Multiple Dimensions

There's a scene in *Star Trek II: The Wrath of Khan* where Captain Kirk moves the Enterprise downward because his opponent thinks in only two dimensions. In fact, most people consider one variable well but have trouble dealing with two dimensions. How many people have fond memories of solving algebraic equations for two variables?

Weak players populate many of the current no-limit hold'em games. Thus, players who master good hand selection and position can win. That is why we consider hands by position next: it is the most important dimension. But if you want to be a consistent winning player, you should also master the other dimensions. If you bet without considering the other players' stack sizes relative to your own, you will be making

15. Sklansky, David. *The Theory of Poker*, p. 16.

a major mistake. You need to be able to exploit your image and the skills (or lack thereof) of your opponents. We cover these issues in the succeeding chapters and urge you to study them. If you don't, you are likely going to leave money you could have won on the table.

Explanation of Position

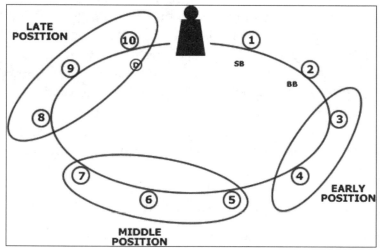

Figure 2: Table Position

Please note that this diagram relates to position before the flop. After the flop, we consider the blinds to be two additional early position seats. Also note that there are several authors who make a distinction with the 3rd seat from the big blind and call it early position, with only the 4th and 5th seats from the big blind acting as middle position. While this is certainly a valid argument, we believe that the difference is not enough to overcome the simplicity of our explanation. We suggest you draw your own conclusion, and take it into consideration during your reading of this book.

There are at least seven situations that you might find yourself in when determining what hands to play in each position. Each of these situations is unique, and each will have a great impact on your hand selection. Pay close attention to these situations, and you will be able to recognize them when they occur. Each of the next three sections on position, early, middle and late, will be broken down by these seven situations. They are:

1. You are first in the pot (after the blinds)

2. There has been one limper before you

3. There have been multiple limpers before you

4. There has been a limp and a raise before you

5. There has been a raise before you

6. There has been a raise and a call before you

7. There has been a raise and a re-raise before you

Several of these situations do not come into play in early position. For example, if you are sitting to the immediate left of the big blind (known as *under the gun*, or simply "UTG"), you will not be facing a raise or multiple limpers. In fact, from under the gun, there is only one situation, and that's being the first to act.

Early Position

Early position is your most precarious position in a poker game. You must be much more selective with the hands you play from up front (the two seats immediately after the big blind) because you still have many players to act after you. Unless you are a mind reader, you need to be careful. One loose call here could trap you for many chips before the hand is over. Often you will see players playing the same hands from any position. In fact, you might be surprised to see one or more players in your game playing every single hand they're dealt. But you know better. You know that position is very important, and when you are one of the first to act, discriminating hand selection is essential.

If you are first to enter a pot, you should be raising with your large pairs: AA, KK, QQ, JJ or TT. With your middle to small pairs 99 to 22, you've got a choice. If it is a loose and relatively passive game, you can limp (calling as opposed to raising) with any pair from early position. In fact, if the game is tight and passive, you might even want to raise with middle pairs like 99, 88 or 77.

With hands like AK and AQs, go ahead and raise most of the time. These are big hands, but they can be vulnerable to many draws, so a raise builds the pot and thins the field, making it unprofitable for many drawing hands to enter the pot. With AQo and occasionally AJs, you can limp. Be warned, however, that AJs is a trap hand (because your jack can cause you kicker trouble); you must be very careful with this hand. If you flop top pair with an ace, don't get married to your hand. It can cost you your stack. There is nothing wrong with folding AJs or AJo in this spot.

If you have limped in early position and it is raised behind you, there are many options you can take depending on the situation. If you have limped with a middle to large pair, you can call the raise unless you know the raiser to be very tight, in which case you will be folding most of your hands to the raise. One situation, however, might change your fold into a call. Say you limped with TT, and the player to your immediate left raises. If three or four players call the raise cold, you have an easy call. The pot is now offering you much better odds, and if you flop a monster like top set, you stand to win a large pot. Similarly, if you have limped with a drawing hand like AQs-AJs, you should usually fold if there are few callers of the raise; however, if there are many callers, especially if the raiser is loose, go ahead and call the raise, but be prepared to fold if the flop is not near perfect for your hand.

If you raise and are re-raised, you should usually *stack-off* (move all of your chips into the pot with a re-raise) when you are holding AA or KK. This is the ideal situation for AA and KK, and you probably have the best hand. If you are holding QQ-TT, you need to be careful. If you know that the re-raiser is loose and likes to make a lot of moves, you can call with these hands, or even re-raise him with QQ and JJ. With the rest of your holdings, you should probably fold. Even AKs is not a hand you want to take heads-up against a re-raiser for a lot of money. There is an argument for calling with AK here, and we don't dispute that, but folding to a large re-raise is fine in this spot. You are most likely facing a large pocket pair, and usually you are an 11 to 10 underdog at best. You should wait for a better situation.

If you have raised in early position and it is then re-raised and re-raised again behind you, put all of your chips in with AA and usually fold every other hand, even KK. The third raise is almost always AA (sometimes KK, but not often).

When there is one limper before you, narrow your raising hands to AA and KK. With QQ, JJ, TT and 99, you can still raise, but it is also advisable to sometimes limp with these hands in this situation. With middle to small pairs (88-22), limp or fold. This is similar to the situation when you are the first player into the pot. With AKs and AKo, you will usually be raising, but a call is also acceptable. With AQs, you can raise or just call depending on the other players in the game. As hard as it may seem, folding AQs in this spot is another alternative, especially if you know the limper to be tight.

Follow the previous guidelines when it is raised and/or re-raised behind you. The only difference with a limper is that there are potentially more players seeing the flop for this raise, thus slightly improving the pot odds of your suited and connected hands. The strength of your hand does not change here, but more players in the pot makes a drawing hand more attractive.

When there is a raise before you, you must tighten up considerably. You will still want to re-raise with AA and KK, and sometimes with QQ, JJ and TT. However, you can also cold call the raise with QQ-TT. Even folding can be the correct play. If the player who has acted before you with a raise is very tight, you can sometimes put him on AA or KK, making your fold of QQ an easy decision. We cannot stress enough how important it is to know your opponents. This is a situation where your knowledge of your opponent might be your only information to make a crucial decision.

The only other hands we recommend playing from early position against a raise are AKs and AKo. You can usually call with these hands unless you believe the raiser to be raising with junk (bluffing), in which case you can re-raise with your AK.

If you have played a hand after a raise, and it is re-raised behind you, fold everything but AA and KK. You should move-in with AA when it comes back to you. With KK, it depends on the action of the first raiser (who initially raised before you acted). If he re-raises all in, fold your kings. If he calls, you can also call. If he folds, you can call or move-in with KK. It is yet one more situation where knowing your opponents is vital. It is not uncommon to have a player in your game capable of raising and re-raising with junk hands. If this type of player is trying to run you over, hands as weak as TT can be played aggressively for a re-raise. Yes, sometimes these players will hold AA (over time, everyone holds the same cards) and you will lose the pot. However, you should play the percentages and in this situation your opponent likely has a worse hand than TT.

There is one alternative play we've not yet discussed: limping with AA. You've probably heard that it is good to mix up your play a bit. We agree. However, AA is a hand that you want to always be raising with before the flop. It is important to get the extra money into the pot when you have the best hand. We don't advise raising with AA pre-flop to eliminate players. On the contrary, with the best hand, you are the favorite no matter how many players enter the pot behind you. The main reason to raise with AA is to build the pot. But what if a player in your game is raising *every* hand? More often than you might expect, someone will sit in your game and raise every hand regardless of the number of players already in the pot. He's trying to run over the game by incorrectly raising with any two cards. You can punish him, however. If you are absolutely certain that he's going to raise before the flop, go ahead and limp with AA or even KK, and plan to re-raise when it gets back to you. If other players are observant, they'll be loosening up and calling raises against this player that they usually wouldn't play, and now you can trap the raiser and the other callers with your pre-flop monster. This is a play that should be attempted only on occasion, but against the right opponents, it is a great weapon to add to your poker arsenal.

However, there is a danger in limping with AA. Let's assume you hold A♠A♣ and are second to act. The under the gun player limps and you also elect to limp. You hope someone raises (and then you would re-raise); however, two other players and both blinds also limp. The flop comes T♥9♥8♦, leaving you with your pair of aces. The small blind bets and the big blind moves all-in. The next player also moves all-in. What should you do?

Hopefully, you would fold. You have one pair—it may be the best possible one pair, but it is *only one pair!* It's almost a certainty that *at least* one of the blinds is ahead of you (not to mention the under the gun player). That's the risk you take when you limp with a big pair. Of course, if someone asks, you folded a pair of deuces.

These are the only hands we recommend you play in early position. As you can see, you will routinely fold in these two seats. Keep in mind, as you watch your opponents play hand after hand from early position, they make many more mistakes per hour than you do, and you are profiting from every one of them.

Middle Position

When in early position, you are the first or second player to act. Therefore, there are few playable hands. When in late position, you are the last or second to last player to act (other than the blinds), and you can take liberties and play quite a few hands. In between lies *middle position*, where caution is the byword and your actions remain limited.

Let's take a look at a trouble hand: ATo. As mentioned in the previous section, ATo causes trouble because if you hit your ace, you may have kicker problems. There are flops you like with ATo: KQJ, Txx, and ATx come to mind. Unfortunately, when you ask the poker gods to give you a specific flop it rarely happens.

This trouble hand remains problematic in middle position. You have four to six players to act after you (including the blinds). Assume you raise with ATo and get called by the cutoff and the button. The flop comes A83 rainbow. You have to act first (a disadvantage) with a hand that has top pair, medium kicker. Suppose you check, wanting to see if one of your opponents bets (showing, presumably, an ace with a big kicker). Your opponents check so you feel comfortable betting the turn, no matter what it is. The turn is a 7 (completing the rainbow). You bet, the cutoff calls, and the button folds. The river is a deuce. You bet again and the cutoff raises. You call and find that the cutoff has 87s.

Now assume you bet the same A83 flop. The cutoff folds but the button calls. The turn is again a 7 (completing the rainbow). You bet but the button raises all-in. You call (the wisdom of the call, or lack thereof, is not the point of the problem) and find that the button has AQo and you are dead to one of the three remaining tens. The deuce on the river costs you the pot.

It is not that you can't win with ATo from middle position; rather, it is difficult to do so. Both of the above situations have happened to the authors. We've learned that saving bets by mucking ATo and other trouble hands in middle position is frequently the winning play. Now, let's discuss some specific situations.

When you are the first player to act, you should raise with your big *or* medium pairs (AA through 88) *and* AK and AQ. As there are fewer players left to act, your standards for raising lessen. As in early position, you want to raise with your premium hands. Medium pairs are now worthy of raises; your goal is win the pot with your raise. One point that should be emphasized is that the amount you raise should be the same no matter if you have AA or 88. If you vary your raises by the type of pair you hold, be aware that your opponents *will* catch on and make fewer mistakes against you.

If you are re-raised, your strategy depends on (1) your hand and (2) who is doing the re-raising. With a premium hand you can either stack off or call with the plan of trapping by either moving all-in on the flop[16] or check-raising all-in on the flop if you are up against a particularly aggressive oppo-

---

16. This play of calling a raise before the flop and then moving all-in on the flop is often referred to as the *Stop-n-Go*, and is frequently a good weapon to use against an opponent who is often out of line.

nent. If you are re-raised and you have a medium pair, you must consider who re-raised you and what he might hold, the pot odds you are getting, and whether you might be able to *bet your opponent off the hand* on the flop.

Betting your opponent off the hand is just that: making a strong bet (at least pot size) with the goal of forcing your opponent to fold. This can only be done infrequently and requires certain conditions. First, your opponent must be a good enough player to fold a decent hand. This play will not work against a calling station. Second, the flop needs to look like it would hit a big hand or it must hit your hand. Third, your opponent must miss the flop—or at least hit it weak enough to be able to fold the hand under pressure. For example, suppose you raise with 88 and are re-raised by the button. You think your opponent has AK or AQ. If the flop comes J73 you can bet as if you hit the jack. Of course, if your opponent holds JJ you are going to lose that initial bet, which is why you must be able to read your opponents to make this play. Obviously, if the flop comes with an 8 you can bet your set.

When there is one limper before you, you must ask yourself what the limper has and why did he limp *before* you act. Most players limp in typical games because either they have a hand they'd like to see a flop cheaply with or they want to trap someone. Usually, a cheap flop is the goal; however, always be aware that a trap may be lurking.

The correct strategy for this case is similar to that of early position. You should raise with your big pairs (TT through AA) and your big aces (AK and AQ). If you win the pot by making the raise, great; if not, you'd like to limit the number of players in the pot to improve your chances. With small pairs (22 through 99), any action may be correct. You need to judge your opponents and determine what the impact of a raise or a call would be. There are even times where folding is correct, especially with the smaller pairs. If you believe that there will be no raise, any pair is worth calling to give you the chance of flopping a set. However, if you limp with, say, deuces and another player makes a substantial raise, you should be ready to fold your hand.

The only trouble hand that we recommend playing in this situation is KQs. We are not fond of this hand. We've lost too much money when a queen falls on the flop and we're up against AQ. However, KQs has the benefit of being "big" and when you do hit the flop, you are likely ahead of a limper. Be aware, though, that many players consider AQ and even AK limping hands and that you should fold KQs to a substantial raise.

With multiple limpers ahead of you, we recommend almost the identical strategy (as to when there is one limper). The only change is that you should almost always call or raise with your small pairs even when there is a risk of a re-raise. The pot odds (for flopping a set) are just too good.

When someone raises in front of you, the number of hands you should play shrinks dramatically. This situation plays almost exactly like a raise in front of you when you are in early position. The only difference is that if you are up against a particularly *loose* player, you can occasionally play your medium pairs (77 through 99). Either raising or calling with these pairs can work.

Let's say that you are up against a loose player who has QQ and has raised in early position. You hold 88 and elect to re-raise, representing a big hand. This situation is almost identical to the example described above (88 versus AK). Of course, there is great risk in this maneuver; your opponent can hold AA. If he re-raises, you are likely in trouble. If he calls, you must play the hand by ear (but *you* have position).

When there is a raise followed by a call in front of you, your pot odds for playing the hand have improved. Thus, you can play more hands than when there is a raise in front of you with no callers. Again, you should re-raise with your big hands (AA and KK). With your other large pairs (QQ through JJ) or AK, you should raise, fold, or call. Raising works when you can either isolate one player (knocking out the potential winning hand) or when you can pick-up the pot right there. However, if you think you are up against aces or kings, fold your pair! You may not get a large pair often, but putting chips into a pot when you are a substantial underdog is not winning poker (you will *not* have the right odds in that situation). Calling may also be the right action. Your call may get other players to call (the *leading the flock* mentality) giving you the correct odds to outdraw your opponents. Calling is wrong, though, when you have the best hand. Again, you must know your players.

With your small to middle pairs (55 through TT), calling or folding is usually the correct action. Your hand is now too weak for a raise because you cannot stand being re-raised. The reasons for calling or folding are the same as when you hold QQ or JJ.

A limp followed by a raise in front of you is played almost identically as to when there is a raise followed by a call. The only differences are that TT moves up in value (it is a large pair) and AQ becomes playable (treated just like AK). The raiser can hold a slightly worse hand than the previous situation, which causes the subtle change in hand values.

Finally, when there is a raise followed by a re-raise, you must play very cautiously. You can re-raise with aces, of course. With kings, either re-raising or folding is right. It is hard to put an opponent on aces. Unless you have the perfect read and put your opponent on aces, re-raise (all-in, unless the stacks are too large to warrant it). Yes, you will run into aces occasionally; unfortunately, it's an occupational hazard. When it happens, all you can do is hope that this hand is the one chance in five that you will win with your kings. If kings cause heartburn when you are faced by a raise and a re-raise, consider what happens when you hold queens. You are looking at two raises from early to middle position players. Unless you believe your opponents are quite loose, it is likely that at least one of them has AA, KK or AK. You are a substantial underdog in the first two cases and in a coin-flip situation in the latter. Folding is often the correct move. If you have a strong read that your opponents are weak, then you can call or re-raise.

Middle position is dominated by caution. While you can play fast and loose, with at least four players left to act you risk running into a big hand. If you have good knowledge of your opponents, the range of hands you can play widens a bit. However, while the hare may win the race as to getting their chips in the pot, it is usually the tortoise that accumulates the chips.

Late Position

How do you make money when playing no-limit hold'em? Do you make it by *stealing* the blinds (attempting to take the pot with hands you would normally fold)? Do you succeed by doubling up with big hand versus big hand (e.g. AA versus KK)? Do you increase your stack by knocking off a big pair when you flop a set with a smaller pair (e.g. 33 versus AA)? Depending on the game, you win by all of these.

As mentioned previously, you can play more hands from late position because you will always act last (or almost last) and have more information. Obviously, you would play AA from any position. Equally clear, 72 should be sent to the muck in all positions. Trouble hands, such as KJ and QT can be played from late position but should not be played from early position.

When you are the first player to act. You can raise with *any* pair, any big or medium ace, and "big card" hands (i.e., KJ, QT, KT, etc.). You should also frequently raise with your small ace holdings (A8 – A2). With only two to four players left to act after you, any of these hands are likely the best hand outstanding. Likely, though, does not mean certain.

Recently one of the authors held A9s on the button in a $200 fixed buy-in no-limit hold'em game. Everyone folded to the author who made the standard raise. Only the big blind called him. The flop was Q74 rainbow. Both players checked. The turn was a nine, completing the rainbow. The big blind made a pot-sized bet. The author elected to raise. After a long hesitation the big blind called. The author bet the river (a deuce) and was called by the big blind who held KK. Remember, the blinds can hold cards, too!

Depending on the game, suited connectors like 8♦7♦ also are raising hands. You are hoping that your raise will steal the blinds. The suited connectors do have attributes if you are called. In fact, your hand is the favorite against two random hands.[17] Remember, that's what the blinds hold—random hands. However, if you are raised (or even worse, raised and re-raised) you should consider giving up your hand against most opponents. You have a drawing hand against either a made hand or a better drawing hand. This is *not* the situation where you want to stack off.

Another factor in stealing the blinds is that the blinds can be quite small in some no-limit hold'em games. If the blinds are $1 and $2, you will have to steal a whole lot of blinds to

17. Based on a *Poker Probe* simulation of 10,000 hands. *Poker Probe* is Mike Caro's poker simulation tool and is available from ConJelCo. See the bibliography for more information on *Poker Probe*.

make a profit (especially in a tight game). However, if the blinds are $2 and $3 (the Southern California standard for a $100 fixed buy-in no-limit hold'em game) winning the blinds once per orbit combined with a few other winning hands can lead to a very profitable session. This is one of the ways no-limit hold'em differs from limit. Stealing the blinds is almost always profitable in limit, but that is not the case in no-limit. Often you will see players making very large raises (sometimes even all-in) just to steal the blinds. This is poor strategy; the only player who will call you is the one who has you beat.

When there is one limper before you, you must ask the same questions as in middle position. Why did the player limp? Is that how he always comes into a hand? Does he likely hold a small pair? Is he a calling station? Can you bet him off a hand? Always think before you act.

The hand guidelines are similar to those of middle position: raise with your big pairs (AA – TT) and big aces (AK and AQ), and raise, call or fold with your small pairs (99 – 22). You can also play, usually by raising, your other big aces (AJ and AT) and your other "big card" hands. Suited connectors, too, are worth a raise against most opponents.

But what if you raise with 22 and are re-raised? *At best*, you are in a coin-toss situation against any *one* opponent. Let's look at a common example. A middle position player limps in a $1/$2 blind $100 fixed buy-in no-limit hold'em game. You raise to $12. The big blind re-raises to $25 and the limper calls. Should you call?

Remember the section on pot odds? There's $63 in the pot (the big blind's $25, the middle position's $25, your $12, and the small blind's $1) and you must put in $13 in order to win that money. Your pot odds are $76/$13, or 5.85 to 1. Now you don't know your opponents' exact hands; however, let's assume the raiser has K♦K♠ and the middle position player has A♥Q♦. Your *odds* (exact chances of winning) are 4.51 to 1.[18] Since the pot is giving you better odds, you should call. You hope to flop a set and either double or triple up. If you miss the flop you should fold to a bet.

Note that the raiser (holding the hypothetical K♦K♠) did not raise enough. This is a frequent occurrence in no-limit hold'em for several reasons. First, many players have been raised on Internet poker where they can hit a "raise" button and the computer will make the *minimum* possible raise. When these players are in games in a casino, they mimic the computer's strategy. Second, people are inherently thrifty and make the minimum raise necessary in an attempt to drive opponents out of the pot. That is certainly one goal of raising (to win the pot). A second goal of raising is to give your opponents the *wrong price* if they call. The raise, in this case, was not large enough to drive out the opposition (see Chapter 4 for a discussion on how much you should bet).

Of course, computing the *exact* odds of winning a hand is impossible unless your opponents show you their cards. You must attempt to read your opponents' hands and make educated guesses about the cards they hold. That is one reason why, when you are not playing a hand (and you will be folding most hands), you should be watching your opponents.

In general, given the minimum raise and *two* opponents, your call was correct. Let's assume that your opponents held the two best hands in hold'em: aces and kings. Your odds of winning the hand are now 6.03 to 1. With the pot giving

---

18. The authors used Steve Brecher's *Hold'Em Showdown* to compute the exact odds of winning. This freeware program is available at http://www.brecware.com/Software/software.html. See the bibliography for more information about this program.

you 5.85 to 1, a fold is correct. However, the difference between the true odds and the price the pot is giving you is so small that a call is not that bad of a decision, especially when you consider the implied odds of your hand holding up. However, if the first player raises to $100 and is called by the second player, you now must call $88 to win $301 (pot odds of 3.42 to 1). A fold is quite clear in this case.

When there are multiple limpers, your actions will be similar to those when in middle position. With your big pocket pairs you should raise; with your smaller pairs you should either raise or call. Theorists have debated for some time whether a raise or a call is correct with a small pocket pair in late position facing multiple limpers. We're not sure they are going to come to a conclusion during *our* lifetime. We use both methods, depending upon our opposition and the game situation, and we recommend you do the same.

With your big aces (AK, AQ) you should raise. With your medium aces (AJ, AT) you should either raise or *fold*. The problem with medium aces with multiple callers is that you never know what you want to see. Suppose you hold AT on the button and face five limpers. You raise and get two callers. The flop is A83 rainbow. It is checked around to you and you are pretty much forced to bet. You are check-raised and have to decide whether your opponent has flopped a set, has flopped two pair (e.g. A8), has a bigger ace, or is bluffing. You really want your raise to win the pot pre-flop so you don't have to make the tough decision on the flop. Of course, if the flop is ATx, TTx, or KQJ you are quite pleased to be holding AT. The type of opposition you face and the likelihood of winning the pot pre-flop with a raise determine whether you should raise or fold.

You can also play your big cards (i.e. KQ, KT, JT, etc.) and suited connectors. We vary our play with these cards and will raise, call and fold depending on the game situation.

When you are facing a raise, you should re-raise with your premium pocket pairs (AA and KK). With your other big pairs (QQ, JJ, and TT), you need to play your opponent. If you believe your opponent has AA or KK you should fold. However, if your opponent is a loose player your hand may be worth a re-raise. This is a situation where you need to play (and read) your opponent.

With your smaller pairs (99 – 55) you also need to consider what the impact of your decision would be. If you re-raise, can you win the pot immediately? Or are you facing an early position raiser who only raises with aces and kings (thus indicating that a fold would be correct)? While you will have position post-flop, holding the second-best hand at the conclusion of the hand is worthless. Or perhaps just calling is the right action. Unfortunately, *each* of these actions is correct some of the time. You will need to use your experience and especially your judgment of the opposition.

With AK, you should either raise or call, depending on your opponent. If your opponent is a loose player you may have the best hand. However, AK versus any pair is a coin-toss. There is nothing wrong with just calling, seeing the flop, and using your position as a weapon. Suppose your opponent holds TT and has raised. You elect to re-raise all-in and your opponent calls. You lose when the board comes J73/Q/8. Now suppose you just call. The flop comes J73. Your opponent checks and you make a pot-sized bet. You are likely to win the hand, as many players will fold to the overcard. This does not mean that calling is *always* the correct decision. On the contrary, you need to know your opponent's tendencies to know whether you should raise or call.

We play AQ quite cautiously against a raise. We will either re-raise or fold the hand, depending upon the opposition and our read.

When you face a raise followed by a call, your actions will be very similar to those when you face a raise. With smaller pairs (99 – 55) we either call or fold depending on our read of the opposition and the pot odds. Additionally, we tend to fold unsuited AQ (that is, AQo); this is a tough hand to play in this situation. Indeed, we will only play AQs (and AJs) with the correct pot odds *and* favorable opposition.

Against a limp followed by a raise, our actions are similar to those when faced with a raise followed by a call. There is a major difference with this scenario: the original limper can re-raise. Thus, we play this situation tighter than the previous case. In all other aspects, though, the two cases are very similar.

Against a raise followed by a re-raise, you must play quite cautiously. Aces and kings are, of course, worth a raise (if you are *certain* that an opponent holds aces, kings can be folded); queens and jacks *may* be worth a raise or a call depending on the situation (your opponents and your reads of those opponents). Everything else, including AK, should find the muck.

When you are in late position, you have the advantage of acting last. However, because so many of your opponents have no concept of position (most players consider only their own cards) you should still be wary. There is nothing wrong with mucking a trash hand regardless of your position. Remember, part of your winnings for a session are the bets you save.

Chapter 6
The Blinds

F act: The typical player loses more money in the blinds than in any other position. The reason for this is twofold. First, you are forced to put money into the pot *before* looking at your cards. Second, you are in the very worst position after the flop. Obviously, playing the blinds is precarious and requires careful consideration.

Before our discussion of hand selection in the blinds, let's address two very important concepts: *blind stealing* and *calls based solely on odds, not cards.*

As discussed earlier, even in a no-limit game, players are going to be stealing blinds—it is the nature of hold'em. Obviously this is not as important in no-limit (because of the small size of the blinds), but it is still a factor. Even though it is only a small portion of your stack (we hope), you can not allow your blinds to be taken at will by anyone with the guts to raise you with any two cards. While your two cards are random cards, you must remember that, if the button is attempting to steal *every* time it is folded to him, than *his cards are random as well.* You cannot allow one player to continually take your blinds. So how do you defend your blinds without losing more money overall? Good question.

One of the biggest mistakes we see players make in the recent flood of small no-limit games is that they defend their blinds *far* too often. Usually, this defense is simply calling a late-position raise. Many players will *always* make this call in either the small blind or the big blind. Those players, we assure you, lose a *lot* of money.

The correct way to defend your blinds is to sometimes call, sometimes raise, and sometimes fold. In other words, you need to be unpredictable. Luckily, the random nature of cards can often make the decision for you. You can muck the worst of hands, call with your decent hands, and raise with your big hands. But often, you will need to call or raise with hands that might not be the best. For example, you are in the big blind with 8♠5♠ and the button is first in with a small raise. Some of the time, you will call this raise. Yes, this is a poor holding and you are out of position. However, the hand does have possible flops that benefit you, and depending on your style of play, you can be aggressive on any number of flops with this hand. Don't take this concept too far, however. Defending your blinds too liberally is a sure way to destroy your hourly win rate. Most of the time, you will be throwing away your junk hands to this type of raise, even if you are certain the raiser is on a steal and has very little.

As another example, you are holding J♥T♣ in the small blind, and the button makes an "annoyance" raise to twice the big blind. As noted before, players who play online will frequently make this "two-times" raise. Many players also feel obligated to make a token raise in this spot to steal the blinds, often feeling weak were they to fold. This is a spot where a re-raise is sometimes correct.

One key thing to remember when defending your blinds is this: always be thinking about getting out of the hand. If you defend your blinds by re-raising and are, in turn, re-raised before the flop, most likely you've got the worst of it and you should probably fold. This is not always the case, but this situation usually indicates trouble. Also, if you've re-raised to defend your blinds and are called, your play on the flop needs to be very cautious. Remember, you are often against a random stealing hand, and his chances of hitting the flop are the same as yours. Don't let your ego take over and cause you to lose half your stack while defending your puny $2 small blind.

The second concept you need to be very aware of, especially in the small blind, is pot odds. This is a case of using pot odds to make a decision on your play *before* the flop, not while drawing after the flop.

Many new players, realizing that tight play is rewarded, will actually be folding too much in the small blind. How is this possible? Let's look at an example. Assume a typical Southern California no-limit game with a $100 fixed buy-in with blinds of $2 and $3. You are in the small blind with 9♠4♦. Seven players limp before it gets back to you. Your hand is garbage, so conventional reasoning dictates that you should fold. Not so fast! Let's run the numbers. Seven limpers at $3 each is $21, plus the big blind's $3 and your $2 already in the pot bring the total to $26. It is going to cost you $1 to call, making your pot odds (if the big blind doesn't raise) 26-1. Do you still want to fold? With these odds (and even much worse odds) there is simply no hand you can fold in the small-blind. Even the lowly 72o is worth a call here. What you are looking for is a monster flop, or a flop that *really* hits your hand. This won't happen very often, but with the odds the pot is laying you to call, you are going to be around a lot more to catch that occasional monster flop.

However, when there are only four or five callers you should fold. The odds the pot lays are excellent (17 to 1 at a minimum); however, there are two negative factors that usually outweigh the good odds. First, your position post-flop will be the worst possible as you must act first every betting round. Second, when you hit the flop well but not superbly, you can find yourself making difficult to impossible decisions. Let's look at one example.

Assume that you hold K♠8♦ in a Southern California no-limit game. You've called from the small blind and six of you have seen a flop of K♥9♦4♣. There's $14 left in the pot after the house's $4 is removed and you are first to act. You elect to bet $15. Two players fold and the next player raises to $40. The other players fold and you must make a decision. Do you fold your king with a mediocre kicker and find that the other player had a king with an even worse kicker? Or do you call (or raise) and find that the other player flopped two pair or even a set of fours? There is no right answer. Instead of answering *this* question, it is better (in the long run) to fold these bad hands unless the pot is laying tremendous odds (e.g. everyone has called).

The key to remember here, just as was the case in defending your blinds above, is to be able to get away from the hand. Say you called from the small blind with that 94o. The flop comes 962 rainbow. It is bet from early position after you have checked, and called in late position. Are you going to call? We hope not. You might have the best hand, but most likely you are in trouble. Any overcard scares you here, and someone might also be slow-playing a flopped set. Make those calls when the pot is giving you excellent odds, but learn to recognize flops that will really hurt you.

Now for the specific play of hands while in the blinds.

The Big Blind

The big blind is often a no-brainer, as you will frequently be faced with the option to check or raise. In these smaller no-limit games, limping is often the norm. You will be seeing a lot of flops while in the big blind with complete garbage hands just because no one raised before you. Sometimes you will actually see players *folding the option* (folding from the big blind when it costs them nothing to see the flop) in the big blind. This is a horrible play, of course, but it is not as rare as you might think. However, if there is action before you, or if you have a strong hand, you will need to make a decision.

If there is one limper before you, raise with your pairs AA-99. You most likely have the best hand. You will also want to raise with any AK or AQ, and usually with AJs. Although calling with these hands is also acceptable, we feel that a raise is the better play. Raising can often win the pot without a flop, but if not, it puts you in the driver's seat on the flop. Check with all other hands.

If there are several limpers before you, raise with AA-QQ and AK. Just check with all your other hands. With multiple limpers, you will want to see a flop cheaply, as it is going to be very difficult to win the pot pre-flop with a raise. The only exception is the special play we'll talk about at the end of this chapter.

If there is a raise before you, re-raise with AA or KK. With QQ-TT, you can re-raise, call or fold. This decision depends on the raiser. With AK, tend to re-raise, but calling is also acceptable. You can also call with your middle pairs 99-77, however, a lot depends on what type of player the pre-flop raiser is and what range of holdings he might have.

If there is a raise and a call before you, you will usually want to re-raise with AA or KK. Often, when you make this re-raise, you will be moving all-in. With QQ-JJ, you have several options depending on the players who have acted before you. You can call, fold or raise here. With AK, as before, tend to re-raise most of the time, with calling being a second option.

If there is a raise and a re-raise before you, re-raise with AA and (usually) KK (this third raise is usually for all of your chips). Folding KK is also an option, but most of the time, you will be putting it all in. The second raise often means AA (not always), and even though you've got a monster hand, you might be worse than a 4 to1 underdog. You can also elect to just call with KK here, but we feel that is probably the worst option of the three. With QQ you can call unless you are sure one of the raisers has you beaten. If you feel strongly that you are facing aces or kings, you should fold. You can, however, re-raise with QQ here, but that's going to depend greatly on what you think your opponents hold.

With AK, you can re-raise, call or fold. Again, your action with this hand depends on your opponents. Most likely, a fold is in order here. AK and even AKs is one of the most misplayed hands in no-limit hold'em, and you want to avoid calling multiple raises with the hand when you are going to be out of position from the flop on.

Another important consideration when facing a raise and/ or a re-raise is where the raises came from. If the player first to act (under the gun) has raised, tend to respect that raise a lot more than a late position raise, as he'll need much more of a hand to raise from up front. Also, if a re-raise has come from the small blind, you are almost certainly in trouble without AA or KK. The small blind needs to have a very strong hand to re-raise as he is in the worst possible position on the flop and beyond. Many players will only re-raise in this spot with AA or KK. Be aware of your opponent's tendencies!

The Small Blind

This is probably the most difficult position to play before the flop in no-limit hold'em. A lot of consideration must go into your decision here, mainly your views of your opponents and their possible holdings. You will be first to act on all betting rounds after the flop, thus, you are in the very worst position. Caution is vital.

Also, as discussed earlier in this section, pot odds can often come into play from this position before the flop. In most cases, it is only going to cost you half a bet (or even a third of a bet) to call. However, there are some structures that make play in the small blind even more difficult, as you will need to call more than half a bet to play. One such structure has blinds of $2 and $5. Although the differences in blinds structures seem small, they are of vital importance: often this difference will turn a call into a fold. Be aware of the odds you are getting in the small blind.

If it has been folded to you and you are first to act, you are in a very fortunate spot. Don't expect this to happen too often, especially with the relatively small blinds in a no-limit game. This is a special case, and you can be much more liberal with the hands you play than in any other case.

Raise with AA-77. You should also usually raise with AK thru A9. With your smaller pairs 66-22, you can call or raise. For example, you can raise or call with any other holding involving an ace, suited or unsuited. Be more inclined to raise with a suited ace. You can also raise with your "big card" hands like KQ-K9, as well as QT-Q9. With lesser holdings you will probably just call. Remember that after the flop, kickers are quite important. With almost all other connectors, including the suited one and two-gap hands, you will usually want to call.[19]

If there is one limper before you, raise with AA-QQ. You can also raise with pairs from JJ-22, but be more cautious with smaller pairs. We also recommend you raise with AK and AQ, but just call with your other big aces AJ-AT.

---

19. A very common practice in this situation is to chop the blinds. Many players, when the hand has been folded to the small blind, feel it's best to just take your money back (if the big blind is willing) and move on to the next hand, thus avoiding or drastically lessening the rake. This is especially true in California, where the rake is fixed, not variable. (See the discussion on size of the rake in Chapter 9 on page 122.) Make sure you clarify your view on this subject at the first opportunity with the players to your immediate right and left. Keep in mind, however, many players will not chop the blinds under any circumstances. These players feel that it is best to play the hand out.

With KQ and KJ, you are looking for a big flop, usually one that can develop into a high straight. Call with these hands, but keep in mind that they can become trap hands. Don't fall in love with the hand if a lone king hits the flop.

You can also call with almost all suited connectors. Again, these standards are assuming that the small blind is half the big blind. If the small blind is more than half the big blind, tend to call more, and if it is less than half the big blind, tend to tighten up.

If there are multiple limpers before you, raise with AA-QQ. You can also raise with JJ-99, but unlike the previous situation with only one limper, you will want to tighten up just a bit, so calling with your small to medium pairs is usually the best option. Otherwise, follow the same advice if there is one limper before you.

If there is a raise before you, you should re-raise with AA-KK. With QQ-TT, you can re-raise, call or fold. As mentioned several times in this section, a lot depends upon your assessment of the other players, especially the raiser. You can also re-raise or just call with AK. Occasionally, you can call or even infrequently re-raise with 99-77. However, in some circumstances folding is correct.

If there is a raise and a call before you, or if there is a limp and a raise before you, re-raise with AA-KK. You will usually just want to call with QQ-JJ. With AK, you can call or re-raise. We don't recommend playing any hands other than these while in the small blind in this situation.

If there is a raise and a re-raise before you, re-raise with AA. With KK-QQ, you can re-raise, call or even fold depending on your assessment of the raisers. Again, a re-raise here will usually be for all of your chips, *so be careful!* We recommend you fold AK in this spot.

A Special Play in the Big Blind

Often, you will find yourself in the big blind against five to eight limpers. When this happens, there is a play you can make for instant profit. Regardless of the hand you hold, you can sometimes make a large raise that will cause all the limpers to fold. For example, the blinds are $2 and $3, and seven limpers, including the small blind, have entered the pot. Thinking it would be nice to pick up the $24, you raise to $30, slightly more than the current size of the pot. Much of the time, you will win without a fight.

Although this is a well-known play, most players just limping in will have a speculative hand (or worse) and won't want to call the raise. Be aware, however, that many players will limp with monster hands like AA or KK just hoping for a raise so they can re-raise. If you use this big blind play too often, you *will* set yourself up for a trap.

Play in the blinds can be a very complicated issue. There are many considerations to make when deciding your proper course of action. Always remember that you are going to be first or second to act on every betting round from the flop to the end of the hand. This is the worst position you can have, and you must be very cautious regardless of your holding.

While protecting your blind money is important, don't take it too far. Often times, a simple blind defense can cost you your whole stack. Don't be afraid to let it go and wait for a better opportunity. Also remember that pot odds play a big role, especially while in the small blind. This simple consideration can often turn a fold into a call.

You lose most of your money while in the blinds; thus, caution is of the utmost importance. Don't get married to a hand that you might raise with on the button. You are in a tough spot, and mistakes can be very costly. Also, don't let opportunities pass to outplay your opponents. You now have several weapons with which to help you in these positions. Use them wisely.

Summary

We have covered a great deal of material in these last two chapters on position. It is highly recommended that you re-read these chapters before moving on in the book. You also might look at Appendix C, which summarizes our pre-flop starting hands broken down by position and action. This may be a useful beginner's tool; however, as the matrix theory states, you need to take into account many different factors into your decision-making process. Not all of these factors can be put in a simple chart. But before you move on to more advanced topics, you will want to have a very good idea of what hands to play before the flop and how to play them. If you've been playing poker for a while, especially limit hold'em, it is essential that you recognize the differences between limit and no-limit in regards to what hands are playable and from what position.

This is one area of your game that, when mastered, will save you the most money in the long run. Small mistakes in hand selection are usually compounded by much larger (more costly) mistakes later in the hand. Avoiding these costly mistakes can be easy if you are playing the proper hands in the first place.

While these chapters are meant only as a guide to starting hands in no-limit hold'em, playing as we suggest will edge you one step closer to winning the money. Over time, you will develop your own style of play, and as you learn to read opponents, you might find yourself playing a little more creatively. That is fine, and we certainly hope you reach that level of play. But never forget the importance of hand selection. Come back to these chapters frequently as a refresher course.

Chapter 7

Play Topics II: Draws and the Play on the Flop

Once the flop comes down, five-sevenths (71.5%) of your hand is known. You may have hit the flop or you may have missed. If your hand matches up with the flop well, many times your play (and betting) will be self-evident. Likewise, if you have really missed the flop, you're looking to either get out of the hand at your first opportunity or you are considering a steal attempt. Some of the toughest decisions come when you get a piece of the flop and find yourself on a draw.

In limit hold'em, you usually have the right price to continue drawing on the flop. Let's look at an example from a $5/$10 *limit* hold'em game. Pre-flop, five people called the button's raise (including both blinds). Assume you know the button holds A♣A♥. You have A♦Q♦ in the small blind. The flop comes T♦8♦4♥. Everyone checks to the button who bets $5. Should you continue in the hand?

This is a pot odds question. There is $60 in the pot before the flop. Assuming you didn't know your opponent's cards, you would have a 35% chance of making the flush. With this "divine" knowledge, you now have a 36.4% chance of making the flush. Your chances of winning the hand are a bit higher, because of *running cards* (the next two cards), at 38.2%.

In a pot odds question you first must compute what you can win. Ignoring (for the moment) implied pot odds, there is $65 in the pot. You can spend $5 for a chance to win $65.

You do not even have to do the math—it is quite clear that you have the right price to draw.[20]

But decisions in *no-limit* hold'em are much different than the decisions we're faced with in limit hold'em. Let's assume a similar problem. Again, you know that the button holds A♣A♥. You have A♦Q♦ in the small blind. The flop comes T♦8♦4♥. Again, five people have seen the button's raise to $10 (the blinds are $1/$2). On the flop, everyone checks to the button. The button bets his entire stack, $150. Should you call?

Now you would have to spend $150 to win $210. The odds of making your hand haven't changed—you'll make your hand 38.2% of the time. But the price the pot is offering has changed drastically: the pot is now offering 1.6 to 1 and you should fold. Of course, we're ignoring (for the moment) implied odds.

Here, in essence, is the main issue of this chapter and the next chapter: when should you call (or raise) with a hand that is trailing but *could* win? We will first examine draws and then look specifically at play on the flop, turn and river. We will also look at some special plays, including bluffs and semi-bluffs.

Draws

The first thing we were taught when we learned to play no-limit hold'em tournaments was "draws are death." The reason for this should be clear—tournament chips cannot be replaced, so playing for your whole stack on a draw is

---

20. Yes, this analysis ignores the board pairing causing a different opponent to hold the winning hand. But for *limit* hold'em, it doesn't matter—there's no way a good (or even average) player would fold in this situation. The odds, by the way, of making your hand are 2.6 to 1. The pot is laying you 13 to 1.

generally not a good idea. (This isn't to say that you should *never* draw in a tournament; that, of course, isn't true. There are numerous situations where drawing is absolutely correct in no-limit hold'em tournaments.) Many no-limit hold'em cash players have come from tournament poker and will rarely play draws because they were taught, "draws are death."

On the other hand, most no-limit cash players have come from limit hold'em where drawing is almost always the right play. Take the first example from this chapter. Would you have calculated the pot odds in that situation? Probably not, because it was clear the pot was offering a great price. Most of the time in loose limit hold'em games, the pot offers a great price (which is why drawing is usually correct). Limit hold'em players have to learn that in no-limit hold'em, the price usually is *not* right.

If you haven't figured it out, the key to draws in no-limit hold'em is knowing if you have the right price. To do this, you *must* know how much money is in the pot. The dealer won't tell you. If you are playing online, the screen will tell you; however, if you're playing in a casino or cardroom, you will have to figure it out yourself. Pay attention to what's going on and this should be relatively easy. Let's look at an example.

You are under-the-gun and fold in a $2/$3 blind no-limit hold'em game. The next player to act calls. This is followed by two folds and a raise to $15. The next player calls. The button raises to $40. Both blinds fold. The original limper calls, as does the raiser to $15. However, the other caller folds. *Quickly,* how much is in the pot? You should come up with $140 by one of two methods.

You could just keep track of the money as it enters the pot. You would mentally be adding the numbers in this fashion:

$$\$140 = \$5 + \$3 + \$15 + \$15 + (\$40 - \$3) + (\$40 - \$15) + \$40$$

$$= \$5, \$8, \$23, \$38, \$78, \$115, \$140$$

Alternatively, you can calculate the pot as the flop is dealt,

$$\$140 = \$40 \times 3 + \$15 + \$5$$

Practice this either by watching online games (and calculating the pot without looking at the computer-generated total) or by watching games in a cardroom.

If you are off by a dollar or two when adding up the pot, it is not a big deal. The goal of this exercise is learning to calculate pot odds; two dollars out of a pot of $100 is a two percent error. If this turns a fold into a call or vice versa, the question is so close that you have a judgment call anyway.

Let's return to the example that opened this chapter. In limit hold'em, calling was absolutely correct while folding is the long-term winner in no-limit hold'em. This does not mean that a call or fold will be correct on a specific hand. Pot odds and their application works in the *long-term*. Suppose you make a pre-flop raise to $20 holding A♣A♥. You were called by the A♦Q♦. The flop is 7♥4♠2♣. You bet $35 and your opponent raises to $150 (all-in). You quickly call. Your opponent must either catch two *running* cards (two of the three remaining queens) to win the pot, or a three and a five to split the pot. You watch in amazement as the turn and river are the Q♣ and Q♠ giving your opponent the pot. Was every action you made correct? Certainly. You suffered the statistical anomaly (or a *bad beat*) when your opponent's 0.30% chance of winning the pot happened to occur.

Now let's change the hand back to the original example, including the original flop of T♦8♦4♥. Again, five people have seen the button's raise to $10 (the blinds are $1/$2). You know the button holds A♣A♥. On the flop, everyone checks to the button. The button bets his entire stack, $150.

The four other players fold and you must decide whether to call with your A♦Q♦. If you call, the house will rake $3 from the pot.

From our earlier discussion we know that the call is wrong. Let's quantify the error using expected values. Let's assume that x is the chance that you will win the hand and y is the chance you will lose the hand. In this case there is no chance of a split pot, so $y = 1 - x$. The expected value if you fold is certain,

EV(fold) = -$10.

You have already bet $10 on the hand and that will be your net loss if you fold. If you call, one of two results will occur: you will either lose an additional $150 or you will win the pot. The total amount of the pot, if you call, will be $357. So the expected value of a call is:

EV(call) = -($150+$10)y + ($357 - $150)$x$

Your chance of winning the pot is 38.18%, or 0.3818. Substituting (1-0.3818) for y and 0.3818 for x and simplifying,

EV(call) = -$160(0.6182) + $207(0.3818) = -$19.88.

Thus, every time you call in this exact situation you will lose, on average, $19.88.

Expected value theory puts put odds into monetary results. When you make a decision that is against the pot odds, you will have a negative expected value (your expectation is that you will lose money); when you make a decision that is supported by pot odds, the expected value is positive.

When you hold a made hand, you want the price your opponents to pay (if they draw) to be wrong. Poker, however, is a game of incomplete information. Suppose you hold A♣A♥ in a $1/$2 blind $100 fixed buy-in no-limit game and have made a pre-flop raise to $12. Two players call you. The flop is T♦8♦4♥. You are first to act. Do you bet? If so, how much? Assume $3 is raked for the house.

Of course you should bet; the only question is how much. If one of your opponents played pocket tens, eights, or fours, you will get called or raised. There is not much you can do about this, unless you *read* what your opponent has (usually based on his giddiness). More likely, one of your opponents flopped top pair or a flush draw. There is $33 in the pot. Why not just bet the approximate size of the pot?

We recommend approximately pot-sized bets (from half the size of the pot to pot-sized) whenever you elect to bet, whether your hand is made or not. If your betting is consistent (in size), there is no way your opponents can determine your hand just by the size of your bet. We have run into opponents who make small bets when they have big hands and big bets when they are drawing, and this makes them very easy to read.

Now look at the situation from the point of view of your opponents. Your first opponent holds J♣T♣ and has flopped top pair. If you were betting an AK, he would have the winning hand. You want him to call for a pot-sized bet because he is a *severe* underdog to beat your AA (3.62 to 1) and he does *not* have the right price to call. If he calls, over time you *will* make money.

Unfortunately, your second opponent has A♦3♦. His pot odds to win the hand heads-up are 1.68 to 1. He had the right price to call prior to the first opponent's call, and now a call is almost a certainty. Let's assume both opponents call and the dealer flips over the 2♠ as the turn card. There is $99 in the pot and you must decide what to do.

Again, betting is clear. You want to drive out one or both of your opponents. If one of your opponents flopped a set it's just not your day. If you strongly believe that to be the case you can check and fold (it is likely he will bet); however, you need to be certain about this because such a move is a decidedly negative expected value play. Again, we would bet about the pot size ($100), unless we had stack-size issues (in which case we would bet our entire stack). Remember, the goal is to cause your opponents to act incorrectly.

Play on the Flop

Many no-limit flops are *heads-up* (two-player affairs). These play very differently from multi-way flops. We'll look at each case and discuss actions when you think you are ahead, behind, or unsure of where you stand. All of the example hands in this chapter assume a $1/$2 blind, $100 fixed buy-in no-limit game.

Heads-Up Flops: When You Think You Are Ahead

Let's first look at a situation when you are certain you are ahead: you have flopped top set. Assume you raised pre-flop to $12 from the button with Q♠Q♣ and only the big blind called you. The flop is Q♦7♥4♣. No matter what your opponent holds, you are the favorite on this hand. In fact, there aren't many hands that your opponent can call a bet with (a smaller set, two pair, or AQ or KQ, and the latter two hands are very unlikely because three of the four queens are out).

You have three possible strategies. First, you can check and give your opponent a free card. Unless your opponent holds specifically 65 (and that's a very unlikely hand for him to have called with pre-flop), this move correctly gives your opponent the chance to catch up. You would love your opponent to make two pair or a smaller set on the turn. In the unlikely case where your opponent bets after you check, you can either call or check-raise (we would probably call to project an image of weakness). One drawback of this strategy is that many opponents are rightly suspicious when they get a free card from a pre-flop raiser.

The second strategy is to just bet normally (a pot-sized bet). Varying your play in poker is essential. If you check every time you flop a made hand, you will get very little action on the turn and river. Some small percentage of the time you should just bet your set of queens. Occasionally you will be called—when your opponent has AA, KK or a small set, for example.

The third possible strategy is to underbet the pot. You are enticing action, making what looks like a "test" bet. Of course, you are testing the waters with a monster but your opponent doesn't know that! (For more on underbetting the pot, see Chapter 4.)

Heads-Up Flops: When You Think You Are Behind

Suppose you hold T♥T♦ and have made a pre-flop raise to $12 with only the big blind calling. The flop is ugly for you: A♣K♣7♣. Your opponent checks. What do you do?

The most likely hand for an opponent to call you after a raise is a hand with an ace. Other likely hands are hands with a king, suited connectors, two random high cards (king, queen, jack, ten), and a small to middle pair.[21]

We are extremely unlikely to bet in this situation. Only if our opponent holds a small pair *without* a club are we likely going to be the winner. His checking in this situation does *not* show weakness. It is standard to check to the raiser after the flop—although we do not advise this practice. You raised and lost—check and pray for a miracle on the turn and river.

---

21. This is *not* a scientific or even statistical analysis. This is our subjective analysis based on what we've seen from playing in numerous no-limit hold'em games.

Of course, should you believe that your opponent really did miss the flop (say you see a resigned look on his face when he sees the flop) then you can and should bet the flop. We advise, though, that this can be a false tell.

Let's look at another common situation when you believe you are behind. You hold 7♣7♠ and have called your opponent's middle position pre-flop raise to $6. You were hoping for other callers but only the two of you see the flop of Q♦8♥8♠. Your opponent bets $10 and you must act.

About half of the time we will fold. If our opponent raised without a pair, we're likely ahead. Unfortunately, there is almost no way of determining that, so a fold is usually correct. If we do not fold, we're likely raising. By making this bluff raise we hope that our pair is ahead (perhaps our opponent holds AK or AJ) or that we can drive our opponent out of the pot. Depending on the opponent, you may have to make two bluffs at the pot in order to win the pot (see bluffing, Chapter 8). Needless to say, this is a high-risk action. If your opponent has a big pair (e.g. AA) or a big made hand (e.g. QQ), you are going to lose quite a bit of money unless you recognize early on that you are behind.

Heads-Up Flops: When You Don't Know Where You Stand

While much of the time you will believe you are ahead or behind, there are many occasions where you are quite uncertain of where you stand. Some of the time you will have raised pre-flop with big cards (i.e. AK, AQ, KQ, etc.) or a medium pair (e.g. 88) but have missed the flop. Or perhaps you called your opponent's raise and hit top or middle pair. Finally, you might have been in the big blind and have seen the flop for free (or for a small raise) and hit a small piece of it. Let's look at some examples.

You raised pre-flop with A♥K♥ to $11 and only the big blind called. The flop is T♥7♠4♣ giving you two overcards and a back-door flush draw. Your opponent checks. Unless we spot a tell warning us that we're behind, we will almost always bet in this situation. As you may recall, when you bet, three things can happen, and two of them are good. If you have a tight image, your opponent doesn't know if you hold A♥K♥ or A♣A♠—you would play both hands identically. Your goal by betting is to win the pot right here. If you are called, you will need to combine your knowledge of your opponent with your reading skills in order to determine the correct course of action on the turn. Many times you must bluff twice at the pot in order to win it. Of course, if your opponent is a calling station you should check the flop because he won't fold no matter what.

Now, suppose you were in the big blind with A♦T♦ and you have called the button's raise to $8. Again, the flop is T♥7♠4♣. What should you do?

It is time for the poker player's favorite answer: it depends. Is your opponent a straightforward player? Then check and see what he does and play accordingly. If your opponent *will* bet the flop no matter what, check to him most of the time. He will bet, and you can call or raise depending on your read of the situation.

If you are up against a weak player (but *not* a calling station), bet the flop because he will likely fold. If he calls, you know he has a monster. If you are facing a very strong player, you should occasionally bet the flop. He will expect you to make the standard play of checking to him. When you bet you are saying, "I have a strong hand and unless you have a very good hand, fold." A strong player will grasp the message and you can get him to fold the winning hand.

The final situation involves when you have checked your big blind (or have called a two-times raise). Suppose you have two random cards in the big blind, 9♦5♣, and have seen the flop for free; your only opponent is a middle-position limper. The flop is J♦9♣4♥. Should you bet or check to your opponent?

You definitely want to bet when you hit the flop in this situation. First, it is unlikely the flop has hit your opponent. While he can have a jack, nine, four, or an overpair to nines, the odds favor him having other cards. Of course, should he raise you must revise your view of his hand.

Now lets change the flop so that you have absolutely nothing: 7♥7♦2♣. Unless we have a tell from our opponent, we will almost always bet (or check raise) this flop. My opponent expects that this kind of flop would hit our hand—why disappoint him by checking? However, if the flop has a preponderance of high cards, say Q♠T♣9♥, it is too likely to have hit my opponent and we would check (and fold to his bet). Yes, we have a piece of the flop, but our opponent might hold hand like Q♥T♥, K♥J♠, T♦9♠, or even Q♦7♠, all of which leave us in a big hole.

In summary, play from the flop on is where your judgment and card reading skills become essential. Always ask yourself, what does my opponent hold? Is his hitting the flop consistent with the betting? Of course, if you're up against a maniac you will never really know where you stand.

Multi-Way Flops: When You Think You Are Ahead

When you are far ahead, your goal should be to maximize your winnings. Here's a sample hand from a recent no-limit game. You hold 7♠7♣ and have raised pre-flop to $12 from middle position. The next player re-raised to $25. The big blind called and you also called. The flop is 8♣7♦4♥. The big blind checks. You have about $70 left in your stack, the next player has around $75, and the big blind has $200. What should you do?

A check is clear. The next player almost certainly has a big hand, AA, KK, QQ, or AK. The big blind probably has a suited ace or a pair (as long as he doesn't hold 65 or 88, you are in great shape). Why not wait and see what the re-raiser will do and act accordingly? If you make a big bet, the re-raiser (and the big blind) may accurately read you for a set and all you will win is the $50 they have put into the pot. On the actual hand, patience is rewarded: the next player moves all-in (he holds KK) and the big blind calls with only A♦8♦! When the turn is an innocuous small card, only the re-raiser has outs (the two remaining kings). The river does not change anything and you triple-up.

Slow-playing in this situation does involve risk. Every so often, a king will fall on the turn or river (or running non-pairing diamonds giving the big blind a winning hand). Yet isn't the risk worthwhile given the strong likelihood of tripling your stack? Furthermore, it is very difficult for a typical player to lay down kings in this situation, so even a bet won't always be enough to scare a player with a big starting hand.

Sometimes, though, it pays to take a smaller profit. Assume you hold 9♦8♥ in the big blind. Seven of your eight opponents have limped into the pot, so there is $16 in the pot. The flop is J♣T♣7♥ giving you the nut straight. The small blind checks and you must act. What do you do?

There are significant differences between the two hands. On this hand there is a flush draw. Also, the flop features high cards (the J♣ and T♣) that limit hold'em players love playing. Other open-end straight draws could be out against you (KQ, Q9). It is almost certain that someone else hit some part of the flop. Slow-playing in this situation would be a mistake. If no one calls your bet, you might have been able to win more had you slow-played. But it is also possible that you would have turned a small win into a big loss. In fact, if one of your opponents holds K♣Q♣, you are *not* the favorite on the hand—your opponent will win the pot 53% of the time (he has 14 outs twice: four aces, three nines, and seven other clubs).

Another common situation arises when you hold AK and hit the flop. Assume you hold A♥K♦ and have raised pre-flop to $12, with the button and the big blind calling you. The flop is K♠8♠4♥, giving you top-pair, top kicker. The big blind, a loose player, checks, and you must decide what to do.

This is a somewhat dangerous flop, given the possible flush draw out against you. It's also possible that someone has flopped a set, in which case you are in deep trouble. Finally, if you make a pot-sized bet (say $35), what will someone call you with? Possibly a flush draw, a pair and a flush draw (e.g. A♠4♠) or a flush draw combined with an inside straight draw (e.g. 7♠6♠). You will be called or raised by two pair or a set. It is not that we think you shouldn't make a pot-sized bet (we think you should); rather, when you are called, ask yourself what your opponent(s) hold. If a spade comes on the turn you need to tread very carefully.

Multi-Way Flops: When You Think You Are Behind

Much of the time when you see the flop, you will either miss it or catch just a very small piece of it. Consider the following hand. You hold 8♠7♠ in the small blind, and threw the extra $1 into the unraised pot and joined five others to see the flop. You were disappointed when the flop came Q♦T♦6♠, giving you an inside straight draw and a backdoor flush draw. You check, of course, as does the big blind. The next player bets $15, and three players call before the action gets back to you. What do you do?

Believe it or not, we've seen a lot of players call in this situation. After all, they have two draws, so what can go wrong? Well, lets examine the merits of this hand: (1) running spades will likely make you the winner (unless the board pairs) and (2) if the turn and river are a 5 and 4 (in any order), you will make the nut straight; however, if either is a diamond, a flush will be possible. Now, lets list the demerits of this hand:

- While a 9 gives you a straight, a higher straight is possible;

- With four players already in the hand, *at the very least,* you are against top pair, and at least one of the other possibilities (a set, two pair, straight and flush draws) may be vying for the pot;

- With two cards flopping in the high card zone (cards ten and higher), you cannot use aggression to force players out of the pot—someone has hit the flop too hard to leave.

All-in-all, a fold is clear-cut.

Our best advice is simple: when you miss the flop in a multi-way pot and someone bets, fold. Missing the pot does *not* include when you have draws to the nuts, multiple draws, and draws combined with hitting a small part of the flop. But the draws need to be reasonable, and you should have a good chance of winning the pot if you make your draws. Remember, the other players in the hand believe that they can win the pot. Always ask yourself what they hold, and why your hand can beat their hands.

Here's another example. You hold A♣5♣ in the big blind. A middle-position player raised to $4, and four players called. Getting pot odds of 11.5 to 1, you call as well. The small blind folded, so you must act first after the flop of A♥T♠2♦. What do you do?

You have flopped top pair, lousy kicker. Your only other "draw" is a backdoor straight draw: a 4 and a 3 on the turn and river will give you a *wheel* (the lowest possible straight, ace to five). That's not much of a draw, and you correctly elect to check. The raiser bets $20, and you fold when it is your turn to act. Yes, you may have the best hand. However, you are out of position and it could cost you your entire stack to find out you were wrong. Prudence demands a fold.

Now let's change the hand slightly: you raise with A♣5♣ to $12 from the cutoff seat and get three callers (the two blinds and a middle-position player). The flop is A♥T♠2♦ and the other players check. Even though you are likely trailing on the hand you should bet. Unless a player flopped a set or two pair, you have an excellent chance to pick up the pot with your aggression.

Finally, let's look at a raise gone wrong. You raise from the button to $12 with T♣T♠, and four players call. The flop is a nightmare: A♦K♦Q♦. However, you are pleasantly surprised when everyone checks to you. What do you do?

There is no chance that this flop didn't hit one of your opponents. Your inside straight draw is next to worthless. Just because they checked to you doesn't mean an opponent isn't lying in wait. Check, and be ready to fold at your first opportunity. Be thankful you weren't raised all-in pre-flop, called, and were then faced with this flop.

Multi-Way Flops: When You Don't Know Where You Stand

Much of the time you won't know where you stand. You might be ahead, you might be behind, or you might even be tied with another player. There are several types of hands that need to be examined: pocket pairs, hitting top pair but with a poor kicker, flopping middle pair with a good kicker, flopping bottom two pair but someone else is betting, middle flush draws, and *idiot-end* straight draws and straights. (The "idiot-end" straight is when you make the bottom of a straight. If you hold 7♦6♦ and the board is T♥9♣8♠, you have made the idiot-end of the straight.)

Many times you will hold a pocket pair and raise pre-flop, but a higher card flops. Assume you hold J♠J♣ and have raised to $12 pre-flop from middle position, and the cutoff and both blinds have called. The flop comes Q♣8♦8♥ leaving you with your pair of jacks. Both blinds check and you must decide how to act.

This is not as bad a flop as it could be—it might seem that an ace usually flops when you raise with a hand like pocket jacks. In this situation, there is a good chance you are ahead and you should bet. Obviously, if one of your opponents holds an 8, you will be called (or raised). A player with a queen has a tougher decision. You could hold kings, aces, or even pocket queens. You will get a call from A♠Q♠ but you are not likely to be called by Q♦T♦. If the flop had been A♣8♦8♥, it's a much tougher decision. If you bet, you will be called by any 8, of course, and by most players holding an ace. If it were checked to us, we would bet; however, we might fold this hand to a bet when the ace flops. If we were first to act, we would bet.

Now let's change your hand to 5♦5♣. You are in the big blind and five players limped so you went along for the ride. The flop came 7♣6♥4♦, giving you an open-ended straight draw to go with your pocket fives. The small blind checks and you must now act.

This is a great flop for your hand. First, this kind of flop *looks* like it would hit one of the blinds. That you are on a draw (it's unlikely your pair of fives is the best hand on the flop) to win the pot is irrelevant; your opponents will *perceive* that you have the best hand (unless one of them has flopped a straight or a set). You should bet the pot with confidence—you'll likely pick up the pot then and there. Even if you do not win the pot immediately you have a very good chance of winning the hand.

Contrast that with a flop of Q♦8♦2♦, giving you a flush draw to go with your pair of fives. Again, the small blind checks and you have to act. While your 5♦ may be the best diamond draw out on the hand, there is no way to know and the odds favor someone else having a better diamond draw. Checking and folding to any bet are the prudent actions.

Let's look at one final hand where you hold a pocket pair. You hold 9♦9♥ on the button. An early position player raised to $6, three players called and you also call. The big blind calls; six of you see a flop of 8♥6♦3♣. The big blind checks, and to your surprise, the raiser checks. The next player bets $20 into the $37 pot, with the next two players folding. You must decide how to act with your overpair.

What does the pre-flop raiser hold? Perhaps he holds AK or AQ and missed the flop. Or he might hold AA and be waiting for a bet. What does the bettor hold? Maybe he has top pair, or perhaps a set, or maybe even an overpair or two pair. In this situation you must play the players. Our inclination would be to fold—there is a strong likelihood you are beaten—but that could be the incorrect action. This is a tough, perhaps insoluble problem.

Now let's look at when you hit top pair, but have a poor kicker. Assume you hold A♣4♣ and are in the big blind. An early position player raises to $4, three players call and you elect to throw in the extra $2 (the small blind folds). The flop is A♠9♥6♦ giving you top pair, lousy kicker. If no one has an ace, you are ahead. But can you really bet given your position? The raiser implied a good ace, a pair, or some other good hand. You have three other players yet to act. A bet *will* pick up the pot when no one has an ace, two pair, a set, or a straight draw. Betting loses when any of those hands are out against you. Checking and seeing what action occurs is your best option.

Now take the same hand with the same flop, except that you have the button. The big blind, pre-flop raiser, and everyone else checks to you. You have an easy bet. Your ace may not be the biggest, but you have position and should use it.

Sometimes you flop middle pair. Assume you hold A♦9♦ in late position. An early position player raised to $12, and four players called and you (rightly or wrongly) also called. Both blinds fold, and six of you see a flop of K♥9♣7♦. The pre-flop raiser bets $50 and you must decide whether to continue with your second pair, top kicker and backdoor flush draw after everyone else folds.

Unless you have a tell, it is hard to call in this situation. The raiser represented a good hand. Perhaps you are lucky, and all he has is A♠Q♠. But he could easily have A♠K♠, K♠K♣, Q♠Q♣, or even A♠A♣. You do not have the right price to call and should fold. However, if the flop had been K♦9♣7♦, giving you the nut flush draw and middle pair, either a call or a raise would be justified.

Another scenario is when you flop bottom two pair but one of your opponents bets. Assume you hold 8♦7♦ on the button. A middle-position player raises to $11, and you, both blinds, and an early-position player call. The flop comes A♣8♥7♥, giving you bottom two pair. Both blinds check, but the early position player moves all-in for $30. The pre-flop raiser then moves all-in for a total of $95. You have about $150 left in your stack and must decide what to do.

If the pre-flop raiser has AA, you are drawing dead (excluding the remote chance of running eights or sevens). You note that the main pot has $115 before you act, and the side pot has $65. If you decide not to fold, you should push all-in with the hopes of preventing anyone else from calling (thus, increasing your chance of winning the pot).

A lot depends on your read of the two players who are all-in. If they are aware players, folding is clear. Examine the actions of the early position player. He did *not* raise all-in pre-flop—there is no way he holds AA given his small stack size (entering the hand). His possible hands are A8, A7, 88, 77, 87, AK, flush draws, and straight draws. Even a straight-flush draw is possible. You are ahead of the draws (except a straight-flush draw) but are drawing dead (or close to it) to all the other hands except 87. Now let's take a look at the pre-flop raiser's hand. He could easily hold AA. If you are lucky, he holds AK or some other big ace (but not A♥x♥). Perhaps you are ahead, but you could easily be drawing dead. Unless we had a significant tell, we'd fold in this situation. However, if we had top two pair, or top and bottom pair, we would raise all-in.

Here's another hand where you flop bottom two pair. You hold 3♣2♣ in the big blind. Five players limp (including the small blind) and you see the flop for free. The flop comes 9♣3♥2♦, giving you bottom two pair and a backdoor flush draw. The small blind bets $10 and you must act.

We would raise to $40. Slow-playing bottom two pair is rarely worth the risk. Assume the small blind holds A9 (or even 97) and you just call. What will you do when a 7 comes on the turn (and the ace on the river, or vice versa)? You should attempt to win the pot here and now, and make your opponents pay the wrong price. The only hands you are behind are a flopped set or two pair. While these are possible, it is probable you have the best hand and you definitely should raise.

Another scenario is when you hold a middle flush draw. Let's assume that you hold 8♦7♦ on the button. A middle-position player raises to $11, and you, both blinds, and an early-position player call. This time the flop comes K♦3♦3♥ giving you a middle flush draw. The small blind, a weak player, bets $20. The big blind and the early position caller both fold, while the middle position player (a good, solid player) calls. There is $95 in the pot, and you certainly have the pot odds to call for $20. However, whether you should or not is debatable. Ask yourself, what do your opponents hold? Presumably, the blind has a 3. But what could the original raiser hold to cause him to *call*? We can think of only two hands, KK and A♦x♦, that would cause him to call. And where do you stand versus either of those hands?

Contrast that hand with the following. Again, you hold 8♦7♦ on the button. A middle-position player raises to $11, and you, both blinds, and an early-position player call. The flop comes J♦T♦7♥, giving you bottom pair, a middle flush draw, an inside straight draw, and a one-card straight-flush draw. The small blind checks, and the big blind bets $55. The original raiser thinks for a moment, and then calls. There's $165 in the pot (you have about $200 left in your stack); how do you act?

This is a much better hand for you than the preceding example. While you really do not want to hit a straight (you would end up with the idiot-end if a 9 came on the turn or river), only three flush draws beat you. Additionally, you have more outs with a 7 or a 10 (the most likely hand for the early position bettor is Jx while the original raiser may have an overpair). You do not want to see an *honor* (jack, queen, king, or ace) on the turn—there is a good chance any non-diamond honor would make you a loser. We would call, but moving all-in at this point is not a bad choice either.

Another scenario is when you flop the idiot-end of a straight draw. Again, you hold 8♦7♦ on the button. A middle-position player raises to $11, and you, both blinds, and an early-position player call. The flop T♥9♥2♣, giving you an open-ended straight draw. The small blind checks, and the big blind bets $55. The original raiser thinks for a moment, and then calls. There is $165 in the pot (you have about $200 left in your stack); what do you do?

This is not a good situation for your hand. There is a flush draw out against you, and while a jack gives you a straight it will be the idiot-end. The only card you want to see is a non-heart 6. All you have is three outs so a fold is clear.

Sometimes you are lucky enough to flop a made hand. Again, you hold 8♦7♦ on the button. A middle-position player raises to $11, and you, both blinds, and an early-position player call. The flop is J♣T♥9♦ giving you the idiot-end of the straight. The small blind checks, and the big blind bets $55. The original raiser thinks for a moment, and then calls. There is $165 in the pot (you have about $200 left in your stack); what do you do?

You are only trailing one hand (KQ), and if one of your opponents flopped it, luck just wasn't with you. We would move all-in. You have a good chance of taking the pot with that bet. Also, there are no flush draws out against you. You may be called by a flopped set (you would be the favorite) or two pair (again, you are the favorite). If you just call, what do you do when the turn is the inevitable Q♣, making all sorts of draws (and other made hands) possible?

In conclusion, when you are playing the flop, always consider what your opponents hold. Act based on pot odds, tells, and logic, not your "gut" feelings, and you *will* be ahead of most of your opponents.

Chapter 8

Play Topics III: The Turn, River and Bluffing

A majority of no-limit hands have no betting on the turn and river. Either the hand is won pre-flop or on the flop, or players are all-in on the turn making no further betting possible. However, there are hands where you must determine how to act on the turn (where draws are still possible) and the river (where you are in trouble if you're still drawing). Again, all examples in this chapter assume a $100 fixed buy-in no-limit game with $1/$2 blinds.

The Turn: When You Think You Are Ahead

Assume you hold A♣A♠ on the button. There were two limpers pre-flop and you raised to $12. The big blind and both limpers called. The flop was A♥3♥3♣. Everyone checked the flop. The turn is the T♥, making a flush possible. Again, everyone checks to you. How do you play your nut full house?

The question with this hand is how to maximize your profit. You are left with two reasonable choices: you can either check one more time or you can make a normal bet. Unfortunately, you are not likely to get any callers if you bet (and you are not likely to get callers on the river if you check and bet the river). We would alternate between the two plays. Both have the same small chance of getting a caller.

Now let's look at the situation where you make your hand on the turn. You hold 8♦7♦ on the button. Pre-flop, a middle position player raised to $11, and you, both blinds, and an early-position player called. The flop came A♥T♦3♦ giving you a flush draw. The flop betting went check, check, bet $25, call, call (by you), fold, fold. The turn was the 5♦ giving you the flush. It is checked to you. What action do you make?

Unless you have a tell that one of your opponents has the higher flush, you must bet this hand (with an approximate pot-sized bet). Your hand is vulnerable if a fourth diamond hits the board on the river. Give your opponents the wrong price to call. Also, you are likely up against two pair or a set; this is another reason to price your opponents out of the pot.

The Turn: When You Think You Are Behind

You hold 8♦7♦ on the button. Pre-flop, a middle position player raised to $11, and you, both blinds, and an early-position player called. On the flop of A♠6♦5♥, the small blind bet $30. Everyone called, and getting the correct odds for your draw, you decided to call too. The turn is the 3♠, making a wheel possible and putting a spade flush draw out against you. The small blind moves all-in for $100. The big blind folds, as does the early position player, while the middle position player calls all-in for exactly $100. You have $200 left in your stack and must decide what to do.

First, you should check the pot odds. There's $405 in the pot, and it would cost you $100 to call. While it is possible that one of your opponents has a flush draw, it is not likely. It is more reasonable to assume that the small blind flopped two pair or a set while the original raiser has a set of aces, a big pair, or two pair. Thus, you have eight outs (four nines and four fours). There are 46 unknown cards, so you have an 8/46, or 17.4% chance of making your hand. The pot is laying you 4.05 to 1 odds while your odds of winning the hand are 4.75 to 1. You should fold.

Another common situation is when you hold AK and have missed the flop (where no one bet) and the turn. Assume you hold A♠K♠ under the gun, and you raised pre-flop to $10. Six players, including both blinds, called you. The flop was Q♣2♣2♦. Everyone checked the flop. The turn was the 4♥ leaving you with two overcards. The small blind bets $20 and the big blind folds. What should you do?

You should fold. Someone has a deuce or a queen. Remember, even a pair of threes beats your hand. If you think that a raise will drive out all of your opponents, then do it. It is not that bad of a play. However, a raise is not likely to achieve your desired result in a game as loose as this. Usually, your best play is to fold in this spot and mentally prepare yourself for the next hand.

Another common scenario is when you hold an overpair to the board on the flop but a flush becomes probable on the turn. Assume you hold A♥A♦ in early position. Pre-flop, you raised to $12 and three players (including the big blind) called. The flop was Q♣8♣4♦. You bet $45, and two late positions players call. The turn is the ugly (for you) 7♣ You must act first.

Assuming you are up against aware players, ask yourself what they hold for calling you on the flop. It is likely that at least one of them has a flush draw. Other possible hands include a flopped set, two pair, or AQ. You have no position on this hand, and you should probably check and fold to a bet. You are beat by the opponents' likely hands, and should be thankful that the club came on the turn rather than the river (in which case you would have even more money invested in the pot).

The Turn: When You Don't Know Where You Stand

Most of the time, you will know where you stand on the turn. Yet, there are hands where your status is still undetermined. Typically, these hands are characterized by small pots. However, one class of hands has doubling-up potential: a battle of the blinds.

When the blinds battle, the size of the pot is usually small. After all, in this situation, the small blind either calls the big blind pre-flop (limps) or makes a small raise. Because the size of the pot is small pre-flop, the flop betting *tends* to be small. However, if one of the blinds has a made hand by the turn, and the other blind either has a made hand or a superb draw, the turn betting can become quite heated. Here's an example.

Two players limped pre-flop, the small blind also limped, and the big blind checked his option. Four players saw a flop of 8♣5♦4♥. The small blind bet $10, the big blind called, and everyone else folded. The turn was the J♦. The small blind bet $30, the big blind raised to $100, the small blind went all-in for another $100, and the big blind called. The two hands were exposed: the small blind had 5♥5♠ and the big blind had A♦8♦. The river was the 4♦, giving the big blind his flush but making the small blind a full house.

Most of the other "don't know where you stand" situations involve small pots. If one of your opponents overbets the pot, ask yourself if this is where you can make a lot of money. On the other hand, is this a hand where you can lose a lot of chips? Take the following situation from a recent no-limit game.

The small blind held 7♦3♦ and elected to throw the additional $1 into the pot (there had been four limpers). The big blind checked, and six players saw a flop of T♠7♥4♦. The small blind checked the flop. The big blind bet $5, two limpers folded, one limper called, the other limper folded, and the small blind elected to call with his pair of sevens. The turn was the 3♣. If you were the small blind, what would you do?

You have hit your hand. If you bet, you are marked for T3, 73, 43, or 65. If you check and see what the action is when it comes back to you (*if* it comes back to you), it is possible you will have more information and can check-raise and win a larger pot. If you choose the former method, you can be raised and wonder if one of your opponents has a bigger hand than you. If you choose the latter method, the turn can be checked around and you not only lose a bet, you give your opponents a chance to catch up.

There is no one right choice here. On the specific hand, the small blind bet $20. The big blind raised to $55. The other player re-raised all-in to $150. The betting returned to the small blind who could call all-in for $120 or fold. We hope you would fold: the big blind flopped a set of sevens while the other player had 6♠5♠ and turned the straight.

The River: When You Believe You Are Ahead

On the river you either have made a hand or you haven't. There are no more draws left. If you have the nuts, the only question is how to extract the most money from your opponent(s). If you don't have the nuts, you are left with two questions. First, if you bet (and here a bet includes a check-raise, raise, and other forms of putting money into the pot), can you win the pot? Second, is it better to fold (or check and fold) because your hand won't win and you can't bet your opponents off their hands?

Many times there is no betting on the river because all the money is already in the pot. However, there are two rather common scenarios you can face on the river: (1) you have been leading at the pot from ahead and are still ahead, and (2) you have caught your draw.

Assume you hold K♠K♥ and raise pre-flop to $12, getting the button and the small blind as callers. The flop is K♦8♦6♥. The small blind checks, you elect to check, and the button checks. The turn is the 2♥. The small blind checks, you bet $35, the button calls but the small blind folds. The river is the Q♣, making your set of kings the nuts. You have two choices: you can check and hope that your opponent has hit a hand, or you can bet and likely win what's in the pot. The problem on this hand is that it is very unlikely that the Q♣ helps your opponent. Again, what could your opponent hold to call on the turn? The likely possibilities include a red-suit flush draw, an open-ended straight draw, slow-played aces, a flopped set, and a flopped two-pair. If you bet, he might call you with one of the latter three hands. If you check, he might bet one of the latter three hands. Again, there is no one correct choice—either strategy will work some of the time. We would lean towards betting because we would, in other situations, bet with hands that wouldn't win the pot and we don't want our opponents to equate a check on the river with a made hand.

It is worth noting here that check-raising on the river is often a difficult tactic to execute. You must be certain that one of your opponents will bet. If there is no bet after you have checked, chances are you have missed out on extra profits. If you read your opponents for hands that might call a bet, go ahead and bet. If you are playing against very aggressive opponents who will jump on any sign of weakness, a check-raise might be in order. However, we caution you that the check-raise on the river is usually not the best option. You will see players attempting to do this all the time, and more often than not, they lose potential profits they would have earned from simply betting.

Obviously, if you are the last player to act and you have the nuts, you *must* bet. Even if the other player left in the hand is a friend of yours, remember, there are no friends at the poker table—you must treat everyone alike. Checking when you are last to act and have the best possible hand is unethical and unprofitable.

Now let's consider a hand where you make the best hand on the river. Assume you hold A♣K♣ and raise pre-flop from under the gun to $12. Three players call (both blinds fold), and you see a flop of J♣T♣4♠. You elect to bet $30 with your straight and flush draws, and one player calls. The turn is the 3♦. You bet $50, and your opponent calls. The river is the 2♣, giving you the nuts. What do you do?

You have been representing a made hand, so you should most likely check and hope that your opponent is chasing the flush. Should he bet, you should check-raise (of course). If he checks, most likely you wouldn't have gotten any more money from him by betting because the only hand that he could call with is a smaller flush.

Alternatively, a case can be made for betting about half the pot. This bet has the appearance of uncertainty (of course, you're quite certain where you stand) and may induce a bluff raise by your opponent. This strategy fails against aware opponents; however, it can be quite profitable when facing calling stations and other weak players.

If we held the same hand on the river but were last to act, betting is mandatory. Again, we have the best possible hand and the only method of getting any more money is by betting.

The River: When You Know You Are Behind

Sometimes you just don't make your hand. Consider the following hand. You hold J♣T♣ on the button. An early position player raises to $7, and a middle position player, you, and the big blind call. The flop is very good for your hand: 9♣8♣3♠. The big blind checks, the early position player bets $25, the middle position player folds, you call, and the big blind folds. The 4♥ falls on the turn. The early-position player bets $40 and you call. The river is the 4♠. The early position player bets $50 and you must decide what to do. You have $200 left in your stack while the early position player has $150 left in his stack.

Had the 4♠ been a club, you would likely have the winning hand. You are left with two choices. You could fold, as it is unlikely that your jack high will win the hand. You could also bluff at the pot. The problem with a bluff in this situation is that your opponent is unlikely to believe that the 4♠ helped you. Your best bet is to fold and cut your losses.

Now let's change the river to the T♠. Assume that your opponent bets $50. In this situation a bluff *could* work. If you raise all-in, you are representing Q♣J♣ or 7♣6♣ (with the former hand, the suits might not be clubs). In order for this bluff to work, your opponent must be an aware player and you should have a tight reputation. If he is a calling station, your bluff has no chance of success. Another factor working for the bluff in this situation is that you have a pair of tens. It is possible (though unlikely) that your opponent has AK (perhaps he has A♣K♣ and was drawing, too) and you are bluffing with the best hand. One final note, bluff-calling all-in (if, for example, your opponent had pushed all-in) cannot work.

Let's look at one other situation where you know you are behind. You hold 5♣2♣ in the big blind. Four players limp in (including the small blind), and you check your option. The flop comes T♠8♠4♥ and everyone checks. The turn is the 2♦ giving you bottom pair. Again, everyone checks. The river is the 4♦. The small blind checks. You elect to bet $10, and state loud enough for the table to hear, "You let me get there." Unless someone has a 4, you almost always will pick up the pot. We don't use this move often, and it won't work online, but it is a quick and easy way to pick up a pot.

The River: When You Don't Know Where You Stand

There are not as many hands where it is unclear where you stand on the river compared to the flop and turn. Many of these hands will be pots that have been checked to the river. A more difficult type of hand is where you hold a small pair and called a pre-flop raise. The raiser has checked the flop and turn, implying that he holds an unpaired AK. Here's an example of this kind of hand.

You hold 7♦7♥ in the big blind. Pre-flop, a solid player raises from middle position to $11, and you are the only caller. The flop is Q♣8♣3♦. You and the raiser check. The turn is the 3♠. Again, you both check. The river is the 2♥. Do you bet or check?

This is a very difficult problem because you are out of position. If you bet and your opponent raises, what do you do? Has he been checking with a pocket pair, such as K♥K♠, or even a flopped set, such as Q♥Q♦? Or does he just hold A♣K♣, and believe because he has position he can raise you out of the hand?

In general, we would make our decision based on the type of player we were up against. The example states we face a solid player. Given this, we would check. If the solid player has a big part of the board he will bet, and if he does not he will fold to our bet. Throwing any money into this pot is pointless. If we were facing a calling station, we would bet because the calling station would pay our bet off with A♣K♣. Against a loose-aggressive player we would tend to check and call as he may bluff his money away.

Now change the hand so that the raiser is in early position and you have called from the button. The hands are the same (you still hold 7♦7♥ and the board is Q♣8♣3♦/3♠/2♥) but now you act last. What would you do if your opponent bets $20 or if he checks?

If the other player bets, you should fold unless he is an extremely loose player. There are just too many hands that beat your hand. If he checks, you should almost always bet, because if a pre-flop raiser checks three times, it's very rare that he will call a bet on the river. You might not have the best hand, but you're likely to pick up the pot.

The final example of this section is a hand that has been checked by multiple players to the river. You are in the small blind and hold 7♦2♦, and when six players limp in you toss in the extra dollar. Eight of you see the flop of 4♥4♦4♣. Everyone checks. The turn is the 3♥. Again, everyone checks. The river is the 2♠, giving you fours full of deuces. Do you bet or check?

It is possible you have the best hand (that would mean that no one has a four, three, or pocket pair). However, it is also possible that one of your seven opponents has slow-played *quads* (four-of-a-kind)—this is a common occurrence. You also lack position on the hand. While a bet could work, we would be inclined to check because there's a strong likelihood that if we bet, we will lose the pot. On the other hand, if no one has anything, our full house will take down the small pot.

Bluffing and Semi-Bluffing

In a recent article in *Card Player*, Carlos Mortensen, the 2001 World Champion, said, "Winning in no-limit is all about bluffing."[22] This is certainly true for tournaments and unlimited buy-in no-limit games. However, when buy-ins are restricted or fixed, the semi-bluff (making a bet with a hand that is neither the favorite nor the nuts but has some chance to win the pot) is king. We need to examine why pure bluffs are not as important in the smaller no-limit games.

A *bluff* is betting with a hand that has no chance (or almost no chance) of winning the pot if you are called. If on the flop you hold 5♠4♠ and the flop comes Q♣T♣T♥ and you bet, you are bluffing at the pot. The only way you can win the pot is by driving out all of your opponents.

Bluffs just don't work that often in the smaller no-limit games for several reasons. First, there are too many calling stations in the game. Second, most players in these games tend to be short-stacked, making calls from them more likely. Third, there are too many bluffs being executed, making calls by aware players more likely. And fourth, unlike no-limit tournaments, if you call against what you think is a bluff and lose, you can rebuy.

Televised poker has caused most of the problems with bluffing in the smaller no-limit games. A well-executed bluff makes excellent television. However, rarely shown on broadcasts of the *World Poker Tour* and the *World Series of Poker* are bluffs that lose—these hands don't make good television. Many of the new players flocking to casinos and online cardrooms "learned" poker by watching these shows. They mimic the loose-aggressive style of players like Gus Hanson without understanding the differences between televised tournament poker and small buy-in no-limit games. The presence of just a single calling station greatly reduces the efficacy of pure bluffs.

---

22. Shulman, Allyn Jaffrey. "Juan Carlos Mortensen: El Matador!," *Card Player*, December 31, 2004. Accessed online at http://www.cardplayer.com/poker_magazine/archives/showarticle.php?a_id=14433.

This is *not* to say that you can't make a pure bluff. If you have a tight image, your opponents will have a tough time with occasional bluffs. Even the tight player, though, cannot bluff out a calling station. Although you may dislike how the presence of a calling station removes bluffing from the game, remember that calling stations are overall contributors to your pocketbook.

Much more important in the small no-limit games are semi-bluffs. Here is an example. You hold T♥9♦ in the big blind. An early position player raises pre-flop to $8 and two players call. You also elect to call (the small blind folds). The flop is 7♦6♥2♣. This is a great hand to make a semi-bluff. If you bet $30 (representing a hand that hit the flop, such as pocket sevens or 76), you are likely to win the pot. Even if you get called you have the inside straight draw. If you have a tell that the raiser has a big pocket pair (e.g. AA or KK), then you should not attempt this semi-bluff.

Semi-bluffs also fail against calling stations (after all, they'll call anything). Care also must be taken not to overuse semi-bluffs or your tight image will evaporate. However, we consider the semi-bluff one of the key weapons in our arsenal.

Of course, you could ask if you should bluff at all. This isn't as dumb a question as you might think. The games today[23] are so full of poor players that we believe you can be a successful player and never bluff. However, if you never bluff you will miss many opportunities to make money. We've shown several examples where bluffs can work.

If all your bluffs are successful, you are not bluffing enough. This does not mean you should bluff calling stations (that's just throwing money away); rather, you should not expect to win all your bluffs. Here's an example of an unsuccessful

---

23. This book was written in early 2005.

bluff. Pre-flop, the first player raises to $10 with 9♣9♦ and is called by four players, including the button. The button holds J♦T♦. The flop comes A♦K♦Q♦. Everyone checks the flop. The turn is the 7♥. The pre-flop raiser bets $20, thinking he is on a semi-bluff. After all, if another diamond falls on the river his hand might be good. The button just calls with his Royal Flush (the other two players fold). The river is the 2♠. The pre-flop raiser makes a $25 bluff. The button manages a call (why he doesn't raise, we don't know). Yes, the raiser lost the money he bluffed at the pot. However, the bluffs sowed doubts in his opponent's minds when the raiser bet at other pots. And the raiser did get unlucky in that he ran into the nuts.

So make sure that the semi-bluff is one of the tools of your game. However, the pure bluff can be relegated to the back-burner as its usefulness is diminished in small buy-in no-limit cash games.

Chapter 9

The House Always Wins

I n this chapter we explore the money that the house takes (and, in one case, gives back) from the table. The house *rake*, or *drop*, impacts every poker game. The rake is the small amount that the house takes for running the game. While the amount taken on a per-hand basis is small, the total is quite significant and has a major impact on the game. Additionally, we examine comps and jackpots.

The Rake

You sit down at your favorite cardroom in a $100 fixed buy-in $1/$2 no-limit hold'em game. The table is nine-handed, and you recognize most of your eight opponents. However, when you play in a public cardroom, casino, or online site, you have an additional opponent to contend with: the house. In most cardrooms there is a drop slot just to the right of the dealer where the house rake (or drop) goes after each hand.[24] Poker is *not* a zero-sum game.

Your home game might be a zero-sum game: if you add up all the money every winning player made and add up all the losses from the losers, the two sums should equate (assuming the house takes nothing). Casinos and cardrooms are businesses and must answer to their owners and stockholders: they must make a profit. Thus, out of each hand, a little bit of money is taken for the house.

---

24. In a few cardrooms, such as Foxwoods, the house rake is placed in the dealers' tray and the drop slot is used for the cash taken from players when the dealer sells chips to them.

That little bit of money can amount to quite a bit in fixed buy-in no-limit hold'em games. Several different rake structures are used throughout the United States. The most popular is a percentage rake: 5% or 10% up to $3 to $5. This is used in Nevada, New Jersey, Mississippi, and several other locations. Different structures are used elsewhere. For example, Foxwoods in Connecticut uses a time charge of $5 per half-hour per player. In California variable rakes are illegal; most cardrooms rake $3 to $4 per hand once there is a flop (if there is no flop, $0.50 to $1.00 is dropped).

You might be thinking that $3 per hand isn't much when no-limit pots can be $100, $200, or even $500. That's true, of course. However, once the house takes any money, there must be more losers than winners.

Let's look at the math. Assume that a no-limit hold'em game has 25 hands dealt in an hour and that $4 is raked to the house per hand. Assume further that you are in a full nine-handed game and that you win $400 in four hours. How much, on average, has each of the other players lost?

The total amount lost is the sum of the amount you win plus the house's share. Or, mathematically,

TOTAL LOSSES = TOTAL WINNINGS + HOUSE SHARE

$$= \$400 + (\$4/\text{hand}) \times (25 \text{ hands/hour}) \times (4 \text{ hours})$$

$$= \$400 + \$400$$

$$= \$800$$

So on average, each of your eight opponents lost $100.

If you are a winning player, the fact that the house also wins may seem irrelevant to you. In reality, it is quite relevant. Every hour the house takes a buy-in ($100) off the table. You, as a winning player, are also removing a buy-in from the table (and putting those chips in your stack). Put yourself in the position of a losing player—can he overcome the rake? Most losing players play a style that, in the long run, almost guarantees that they will lose.[25] So they lose, reach into their wallets and rebuy. And rebuy some more. Eventually they run out of money and head home.

What happens when they tell their spouse or significant other that they lost $300 playing poker? Perhaps nothing the first time; however, sooner or later the spouse says either win or stop playing. The fixed buy-in, no-limit hold'em games were introduced in Southern California fifteen months ago (at the date of this writing). Already we're seeing the second to third group of losing players. Fortunately for the winning players, television continues to create new (usually losing) players. However, there is a finite population and sooner or later the games will tighten up. Turning a profit will then become much more difficult.

Today, the winning player can overcome the house rake in most situations. However, there are *virtually unbeatable* situations that we consider to be unplayable. For example, both of the authors recently played at an east coast casino that was breaking in new dealers. The dealer at our table was dealing, *at best,* ten hands per half hour. We were paying a time charge of $5.00 per half hour. Unless you are blessed with miracle cards, such a game is *not* beatable. Once we realized the situation wasn't going to improve, we voted with our feet: we got up and played in a different game where we had a chance to make money.

-----

25. The situation is much worse in small ($3/6 - $6/$12) limit hold'em games. In these games the rake tends to be the highest and the play tends to be the worst of any game in the casino. While you can win in some of those games, it may not be possible for *anyone* to win (in the long run) in *tight* small limit hold'em games because of the house rake.

As we have mentioned, not every player you will encounter is playing to make money. Many play solely for the entertainment value. Do not begrudge your opponents as to *why* they are playing. And don't get upset that the house has to make money. The house has significant overhead: dealers, floor staff, security, chip runners, and maintenance staff. Even online cardrooms have numerous costs: marketing expenses to bring in new players, server and bandwidth costs, customer service and support, as well as anti-collusion programs and personnel.

Tipping

When you play in a public cardroom or casino, you will be interacting primarily with two sets of casino employees: dealers and floorpersons. The floorman will seat you at a table and is responsible for rulings (dispute settlements) in the cardroom.[26] Dealers are responsible for keeping the game moving, awarding each pot, and enforcing the rules. Dealers are not well paid. In fact, their salaries are just above minimum wage. Dealers make up for their low base pay by receiving tips from players.

In no-limit hold'em, when you win a pot of reasonable size, it is customary to tip the dealer $1. If you win a very large pot you should tip a larger amount. However, if you raise and just pick up the blinds, no tip is expected (tipping $1 when you have won $3 does not make much sense). Yes, tipping is another form of the rake. You might argue that the cardrooms should pay their dealers more so that tipping wouldn't be necessary. If they did, the rake would almost certainly be higher.

---

26. In some casinos, the *brush* (the person running the sign-up lists) seats players.

We also believe that you should tip floor personnel and chip runners. While floor personnel receive higher salaries than dealers, they are by no means lavishly paid. If you tip them, you will likely receive better treatment from them. If a seat opens in two games at the same time and you are first on the list, wouldn't you like to be seated in the better game? We guarantee that the floorman knows which game is better.

Tipping is something that Internet players do not have to deal with: the dealer and floorman are just images on a computer screen. Whether you should play online or not is another question. While Internet players do not tip, there are more hands played per hour online. The net cost of playing online or in a brick and mortar casino is probably similar.

Comps

Many cardrooms and casinos provide complimentaries, or comps, to their players. Most require a player to get a casino slot club or poker club card. These cards are almost always free; the cardroom staff at your casino can tell you how to obtain the card. Your card then gets scanned when you sit down in a game and when you leave (alternatively, some cardrooms scan your card every hour). What you can receive depends on how many hours you play.

For example, as of this writing, the Bicycle Casino in Southern California gives players in their no-limit hold'em games $3.00 per hour of play after the first 25 hours in a month (they give $25 for the first 25 hours). Others award a small dollar amount per hour of play (both the Orleans Casino in Las Vegas and Foxwoods in Connecticut do this). Many Las Vegas poker rooms offer a poker room rate for those who play a certain number of hours. On the other hand, some cardrooms offer little but free drinks to players. It never hurts to ask what is available.

Jackpots

In some cardrooms, *bad beat jackpots* are awarded when a rare hand (e.g. Aces full of tens or better) is beaten by a rarer hand (e.g. four-of-a-kind or better).[27] Most jackpots are funded by a small drop taken out of each pot (usually $1.00). Jackpots are normally paid to the players at the table where the jackpot is hit; one payout method awards the loser of the hand 50% of the jackpot, with the winner of the hand receiving 25%, and the other players dealt in splitting the remaining 25%. Jackpot amounts can become quite large, reaching $50,000 to $100,000. Unfortunately, jackpots are *not* a good thing for winning players.[28]

Jackpots take money out of the poker economy. First, the house retains a small percentage (usually around 15%) of the jackpot drop as an administration fee. This money is gone from the poker economy for good. Second, ask yourself what happens when someone wins a large jackpot? Do they gradually put the money back into the game, or do they take their $25,000 and buy a car or take a vacation?[29] Consider the jackpot drop as just another form of house rake.

You should almost *never* play cards pre-flop solely for a jackpot. For example, suppose you hold 3♣3♥ in late position in a new $100 buy-in no-limit hold'em game. Assume that

---

27. Most casinos require that both hole cards from both players play. For example, if the board is K♠K♥K♦A♣A♠, and one player holds A♥A♦ and the other player holds K♣5♣, there would *not* be a jackpot (the quad kings must use an ace on the board as a kicker and can't use his five).
28. Please note that the authors dislike player-funded jackpots. If the jackpot is funded *exclusively* by the house, this becomes more of a "sweepstakes" or giveaway. Getting something from the house for no cost when you lose with a big hand is fine.
29. One of the authors won a jackpot several months ago and used the money for home repairs, a new entertainment center, and for savings.

an early position player raises to $14, and a middle position player re-raises to $30. Do you really want to call $30 when your best-case scenario is to be in a coin-flip situation, and the likelihood of being involved in a jackpot hand is extremely small?

However, after the flop there are occasions to play for the jackpot. Suppose you hold 3♣3♥ in the big blind and get to see the flop for free. You are shocked when you flop quads: the flop is K♦3♦3♠. If there were no jackpot you would check to allow your opponents to catch up. The jackpot just gives you another reason to do so. Yet time and time again we see players seeing flops for the wrong price *solely* because of the jackpot. Do not fall into that trap. If you play enough hands eventually you will be at a table when a jackpot is hit.

We live in a society where many believe you can get something for nothing. That is *never* the case in any casino or cardroom. Comps, jackpots, and other promotions must be paid for. Take advantage of the comps your cardroom offers. If you are lucky enough to win a jackpot, celebrate with your friends and family. Just remember that *every* time you a win a pot the house *will* have already taken its' share.

Chapter 10
Managing Your Mind

Poker is a mental game. Success does not depend on how high you can jump, how fast you can run or how much you can lift. Psychological maneuvering, assessing your opponents, recognizing situations, and creating deceptions key your success in poker. It is the science of decision making that you must master if you want to go home with the money. All of these decisions occur in your mind, of course. It stands to reason that your "training" needs to be mental.

Reading poker books, watching videos of players and tournaments, discussing the game with friends and online— these are all great ways to train your brain and become a better poker player. The more you think about the game away from the table, the better you will become. But, there is one more area of this mental training you might not have considered.

Your emotions, regardless of how tough you are, can take over when you are the most vulnerable. This point is different for everyone, but when it is reached, it can be devastating. You have no doubt seen players on tilt. They play too many hands, make hopeless bluffs again and again, and call in spots where everyone in the room knows they cannot win. It is a disaster, and it can happen to anyone. But how do you avoid the tragedy of tilt? How can you stop the freight train that might have started with a bad beat or a bad player who now has half your stack?

You need to manage your mind.

So what does it mean to manage your mind? Simply this: you must be able to control your emotions in a poker game. If you can achieve this one aspect of poker, you're ahead of almost everyone you will encounter across the felt and, chances are, you will come out ahead.

Avoiding Tilt

In the poker classic *Shut Up and Deal*, Jesse May writes, "And it's tough keeping yourself under tight control night after night, which is why in the gambling world there's an entire vocabulary for losing control."[30] Tilt. Steaming. Losing it. Whatever you want to call it, keeping your emotions away from your decision-making can mean the difference between success and failure while playing.

Tilt usually occurs, not from one isolated event, but by a series of beats that accumulate in the mind like mental toxic waste. With each bluff gone bad or river suckout, anger and hurt take over where rational thought once resided, and coherent thoughts and actions get thrown out the window.

Occasionally you will find a player who just cannot handle any type of beat or loss at all. This player goes on tilt immediately, and regardless of how good he had been playing up until that point, his night is now shot. There are also players who seem to let nothing get under their skin. Nasty beats, taunting and endless re-buys won't ruffle the feathers of this bird. He is a rare breed indeed, as most of us lie somewhere in between these two extremes. One bad beat is not enough to send the average player off his cheese, but six or seven in rapid succession can easily turn a winning night into a symphony of errors, eventually resulting in the destruction of his bankroll.

---

30. Jesse May, *Shut Up and Deal*, p.140.

Avoiding tilt will be more difficult for some than for others. No, we are not immune to tilt. We are human and, on occasion, we need to step away from the game to avoid impending disaster. But with practice, this becomes less and less of a problem for the experienced player, and we hope it will for you as well. Here are some techniques we have used to avoid tilt:

1. After a nasty beat or loss, step away from the table immediately and take a walk. Yes, this sounds a bit silly at first, but the sooner you get up and walk it off, the better it will be for you. If you are especially bothered by losing a particular hand, you need to take a break, regroup and re-focus your mind. This will enable you to forget about the loss a lot faster than had you stayed at the table stewing in your anger.

2. Take frequent breaks. It is important to stay fresh while in a poker game. While your opponents may remain in their seats hour after hour, you will be getting up regularly, stretching your legs, getting fresh air, splashing cold water on your face, or doing some other quick activity that keeps you alert and focused. You do not need to suffer a bad beat to take a time out.

3. Do not play when tired. Sleep depravation will play havoc on the emotions. When the brain doesn't get the required REM sleep, it tends to short-circuit a lot easier, and emotions are quick to jump into the cockpit and grab the controls. Further, being tired or sleepy will eventually cause you to do stupid things like misread your hand or miss an obvious tell. (See also our comments on dealing with tired opponents beginning on page 12 in Chapter 2.)

4. Do not bring your problems to the table. Everyone goes through problems from day to day. Regardless of

what those problems are, you just cannot afford to bring them to the table. If you have just had an argument with your spouse over money, if your kid's teacher just called to discuss his grades, or if your boss is breathing down your neck about working more overtime, you probably shouldn't be playing poker today. Sure, it is just a short drive to the card room, and for some, it is a matter of turning on the computer. However, it is not a good idea to play poker when you have got other things on your mind to worry about. As Roy West likes to say, "Play happy or don't play."[31]

5.   Do not play with someone who rubs you the wrong way. If you have a personal vendetta against someone before you even sit down to play, you are going cause yourself frustration if you try to isolate and beat that player. Before you know it, you will have beaten yourself.

Tilt is a dangerous animal. Like drugs or alcohol, it can make you do things in a game that you normally wouldn't do. If you are going to succeed at poker, you need to play your A-game most of the time. Tilt takes you off that by at least a few letters. Preventive measures taken to avoid tilt before you sit down to play will give you at least a fighting chance against what some players lovingly refer to as the "bonkers monster."

While we do not advocate specific stop-loss and stop-win amounts, we believe that it is crucial to recognize your threshold of pain. If you are losing in a session, and it seems like no matter how good a hand you hold, you cannot win, it is time to call it a day. You do not quit because you have lost a certain amount, however. You stop playing because

---

31. Roy West, *7 Card Stud: The Complete Course in Winning at Medium and Lower Limits*, p. 95.

that amount is impacting your game and the way you play. Whether you are aware of it or not, large losses impair your judgment in small ways, and the edge that you once enjoyed over your opponents slips away.

Large losses can induce tilt. You may become so afraid to lose with your pocket queens that you do not raise before the flop and, even though there is nothing on the board that appears threatening, you just check and call to the river. Or perhaps you have decided to add a little deception into your game, and now you raise with any two suited cards or any ace with a kicker 5 or higher. This is deception all right— you are deceiving *yourself*. If you recognize any behavior like this, pack it up. Tomorrow is another day. The card room will be there tomorrow and the next day and the next. There is no reason to play when you are not in the right frame of mind.

Is there a point that you should quit after winning a large amount? Perhaps, but again, it is not because of the amount, it is because the amount won might be affecting your play. If you have been playing in a $200 fixed buy-in game for five or six hours, and you have built your stack up to $1,200, you will most likely be inclined to loosen up your play. When you start calling raises cold with hands like A♦4♠ and K♥3♥, you are playing too loose. You can rationalize this play by telling yourself that another $10 pre-flop is nothing (compared to your monster stack), but it is a great way to trap yourself for a much bigger portion of that stack. Three or four of those hands and you might find yourself with a small stack once again.

On the other side of the coin, you might also find yourself playing too tight when you have a big stack. You may want so badly to protect your big win that you do not want to get involved with any hands but aces or kings. While playing tight is usually a good strategy, you are playing too tight now, and you are passing up opportunities to increase your profits.

Sometimes, it is just nice to book a win. If you have been in a slump lately, and nothing you seem to do works out well (poker wise), sometimes it feels great just to get up as soon as you have booked a win—even a small one. We do not advise getting up and leaving when the game is good and you have no personal problems, but we cannot fault a player for quitting "early" and booking that win if the short-term psychological benefits warrant it. If that one win will break your mental slump, it might be a good idea to occasionally hit and run.

Mental and Physical States

So far we have discussed tilt and how to avoid it. We've talked about a few things you can do to prevent it from happening. Yet there are other areas seemingly not related to poker that can have a huge impact on your game.

In one of our tips, we discussed the problem with bringing your personal problems to the table. Good mental health will go a long way in helping you become the best poker player possible. Most people have issues that have caused them problems in the past, and many people still harbor these issues inside. Do you suffer from depression or anxiety? Do you have a substance abuse problem? Perhaps your problems are only temporary, such as a divorce or coping with the death of a loved one.

Regardless of your problems, you should try to deal with them first before becoming serious about the game of poker. This game is mentally and emotionally taxing. The emotional highs and lows are often the equivalent of a psychological amusement park. Poker emotion does *not* mix well with pre-existing mental trauma. For some, poker can be a relaxing and enjoyable activity, but for others, the pitfalls of the game can send them deeper into depression and emotional despair.

This is especially true if you are one of the millions of people all over the world who have addictive personalities. Poker is gambling. Period. For those of us who study and practice poker, it is more of a skill game than gambling; however, the element of gambling remains. If you have a compulsive gambling problem, we strongly recommend against jumping into no-limit poker.

While we are not trying to dissuade you from playing poker, we are trying to convey the fact that if you already have serious problems in your life, poker has the potential to compound those problems if one is not diligent and dedicated to playing well. If you are looking to gamble, we recommend you find another outlet. The chances for huge losses in no-limit hold'em are just too great.

While mental states are often overlooked when it comes to poker, even more neglected are player's physical states. In order to play effectively, you need a healthy and agile mind. With a healthy body, a healthy mind usually follows. Now, we are not saying that a few extra pounds will dull your mind, but it is important to maintain physical health for success in all aspects of your life, and poker is no different. Long hours at the table require a great deal of stamina, both mental and physical. We strongly believe the two states are connected.

So what sort of physical training is required to be a great poker player? Not much, actually. We advise healthy eating, getting plenty of exercise[32] and the right amount of sleep

---

32. Before commencing an exercise program, make sure you discuss it with your personal physician.

when you can. These few simple steps will increase your energy as well as your quality of life. This leads to happiness, and happy poker players usually take down the money.

There are a few physical states you want to avoid:

1. Playing while tired. The mind needs to remain alert and focused, but if you are exhausted from sitting in the same game for the last ten hours, it is probably time to get up. Whether you realize it or not, your decision making is not as sharp as it was when you started, and one lapse in judgment can cost you your whole stack.

2. Playing while sick. Ignoring for a moment the fact that, if you are sick with a virus, you are passing your germs around to your fellow players with each chip you handle, imagine how it impacts your game. If a lack of sleep slows your judgment, feeling under the weather will slow *and* impede your judgment. A wounded body is a wounded mind. When sick, stay home.

3. Physical injuries. Not all physical injuries fall under this category. However, if your particular injury is causing you constant pain, it is best not to play poker. Physical pain constantly takes your mind away from the task at hand. Pain also causes one to become irritable and impatient. From a bad back to a sprained wrist, if you are under any sort of physical pain that is strong enough to be a nuisance, stay out of the card room until you are healed.

4. Drugs and alcohol. We are not writing this book to preach the evils of certain substances. However, we will re-state the obvious side effects of these recreational chemicals. If something causes your brain to do things it wouldn't normally do, or if your thought process is impaired in any way, you shouldn't be at the

poker table. Being drunk or high can also decrease your level of concern for your own bankroll. While being fearless is sometimes a good thing in no-limit hold'em, we do not advise the use of drugs or alcohol to achieve such a state.

You can do all the reading and practicing and discussing you want, but if your physical and mental states are not in line with each other in a harmonic balance, you will severely limit yourself in your quest for poker greatness. Take the time to focus, concentrate, and get in touch with your mind, and do not play if something is amiss. Your body is excellent at giving you clues, and like any good poker player, you just need to know how to read them. Picking up a tell on your opponents is a great skill, but reading *yourself* is possibly the greatest skill of all.

Chapter 11

Managing Your Game

n *Hold'em Excellence*, Lou Krieger said, "If you are serious about poker, you have to treat your game like a business or a profession."[33] While you may only be a recreational player, we feel that managing your game away from the table is just as important as what you do at the table. Not only should you think about the game in the middle of a hand, you need to take steps outside the microcosm of the situation and into your daily life.

Before we get into detail about game management, please do not interpret the above as a recommendation to become obsessed with poker. An expert poker player maintains a solid balance between the game and other facets of life. However, it is essential to your success that you study, take notes, keep records and think about hands away from the table when your mind is fresh. Doing this will allow you a different perspective of a situation, and perhaps you will learn just as much about your game away from the felt as you do riffling a stack of chips and staring at the guy across from you.

We recommend seven specific actions you can take away from the table that will vastly improve your game. They are:

1. Taking Notes
2. Thinking
3. Reading
4. Keeping accurate records
5. Keeping a poker journal

---

33. Lou Krieger, *Hold'em Excellence: From Beginner to Winner*, p. 133.

6.   Maintaining a proper bankroll

7.   Taking vacations

Taking Notes

Have you ever been in the middle of a hand and noticed that a player made a move that you have seen him make before? Sure you have. We often see players following a rigid set of guidelines (often incorrect) during a hand. The observant player will know that these patterns can lend a strong degree of predictability to a player. Often these repetitive plays will have the net effect of giving one's hand away as if the cards were turned face up.

This phenomenon is especially true in no-limit poker, as the size of the bet often determines the exact strength of the hand. You might notice Kevin betting a third of the pot when he has top pair with a weak kicker (perhaps because he'd like to see the turn but doesn't want to call a larger bet). With a stronger kicker or two pair, he bets the exact amount of the pot. With a monster, like a flopped set, he always looks to check-raise. Further, when he check-raises on the flop, it is never a bluff.

Imagine the power of this knowledge. You can almost always put Kevin on a hand if you know his betting patterns (if, of course, he remains true to them). Granted, it is not always this clear-cut. But with keen observation, you will be amazed at the patterns you can pick up on each player you play against. If you are playing in a regular game with the same group of players week after week, your edge will be tremendous if you know the tendencies of the players.

Alright, so Kevin likes to check-raise his monsters on the flop, Wes frequently calls small bets to the river on a draw even if the odds do not warrant it, and Liz is always aggressive with second pair on the flop, but slow-plays her stronger hands. How can you retain all of this knowledge? You write it down, of course. It is not uncommon for a pro to have notes on many of his opponents. These notes can be studied away from the table just before game time, preparing the player for opportunities to exploit his opponents' habits. Keep a small notebook of players, and record everything you see. You will build up quite a file for each player if you are diligent.

A good method of note taking is to mentally capture a thought or two on a player during the game or a hand. The next time you excuse yourself from the table "for a bathroom break or some fresh air," whip out your notebook and jot down your observations. You can rewrite and review them away from the table at a later time.

If you are an online player, you most likely have a note-taking tool built right into the software you are using. *Take advantage of that!* It couldn't be easier, and your notes are right there by the players the next time you face them, all typed and easy to read. Make it your goal to take at least one note for every player at your table during your session. If you strive for that, you will find yourself constantly taking notes. Before you know it, you've got multiple notes on every player.

Another useful and less stressful method of note taking online is "railbirding." Login to your favorite online poker site, go to a table and just watch and take notes without playing. You will find it easier to take notes, and the quality of your observations will most likely be improved. You are not looking through the fog of the game you are involved in this time. You are just a silent observer getting to know your opponents. Once you have built up a nice base of player notes, most of the work will be done, and you can realize the full benefit of your work as you play.

Do not be afraid to change your notes on a player. Perhaps the first time you played with Kevin he was loose and aggressive, but this time you've noticed that he's playing a lot tighter and is conservative with his drawing hands as opposed to jamming every chance he gets. Players do play differently from time to time. Learn to notice odd behavior from players you thought you had a line on. Note what is different and why you think they are playing differently than expected today. Was Kevin just drinking last week? Was he angry about something? So many exterior factors can have a profound effect on a player's game. You need to be aware of such factors and adjust your notes accordingly.

Taking notes on players, as we have seen, can be a huge benefit to your game. Most players you will be playing against in these small no-limit games do not take notes of any kind. They see it as too much work and not worth the effort. The difference is, they are just gambling, and you are playing poker to make money. Taking notes puts you one large step ahead of the pack, and when you lay down your flopped top two-pair to Kevin's check-raise, he'll never know how you could get away from your hand. But you will.

Thinking

Thinking. It sounds easy, doesn't it? So simple. The truth is, it *is* simple—if you know how to do it. When you are away from the table, perhaps at a stoplight or in the waiting room at the doctor's office, it is easy to fantasize about winning huge pots with your rivered straight flush over some poor schmuck's flopped quads. It is the glory of poker; the moments we all imagine will happen someday. The thought of stacking and racking a mountain of green, black and purple chips: it is fun to dream, but is it constructive?

Thinking about the game and daydreaming about impossible scenarios are two very different things. Sure, it is nice to get away from the grind once in a while and take a mental vacation. It helps us get through the tough parts of our day and makes us smile. However, does it improve our game? Perhaps. If it improves our state of mind before a session, or if it helps us ease the strain of tilt, then yes, it helps our game. But for the most part, the kind of thinking you need to do away from the table is entirely different.

One of the best mental exercises you can do while you are not in a game is to re-construct the play of a specific hand. Put yourself in the hand again, and try to notice everything going on at the table. Try to recall the betting, the looks on their faces, the exact cards, and how you played the hand. In this moment of clarity away from the game, you will often find that you have missed something entirely. You may re-member some little clue that would have changed the way you played the hand, and would have saved you a lot of money. Did you play the hand right pre-flop? How about on the flop? On the Turn? The River? Did you over-bet or un-der-bet when you should have done the opposite? Did you make a call when you should have known you were beaten or didn't have the odds to draw? Did you notice a tell but not act on it?

By replaying the hand over and over in your mind, you can identify any errors you made. Make a mental note, or better yet, write it down in your journal (discussed later in this sec-tion). The more you focus these errors, the more likely you are to overcome them. The same can be said of your expert plays. Record those as well, and never forget them. By rec-ognizing and remembering the bad plays as well as the good, you develop habits that take your game to the next level. You become aware of the mistakes *as you make them*, and you will be able to stop and think before you act. Over time, you will notice your bad plays start to diminish and your good plays become amplified.

It often helps to have a friend to talk to about a session or a hand (especially if your friend is in the game). Bouncing your ideas and situations off of other players is another excellent way to gain insight to a particular situation. Poker is a game of constant learning. Although there are players who have volumes of poker knowledge tucked away in their brains, not one of them knows everything. Make it a habit to constantly learn by reviewing hands and asking questions. An experienced friend can be a great resource. He knows what you are going through, as he's been there before. Think of him as your poker mentor. There is no shame in taking on the apprentice role for a while during your long learning process. Almost every great player has had a person (or several) in their lifetime that they went to for poker advice. If you can find an individual like this, you will have turbocharged the learning process.

But please, refrain from telling your mentor any bad beat stories. He's heard them all before.

Reading

As avid readers, this came naturally for us. But some of you might not enjoy reading books as much as we do. That's fine. However, if you really want to gain an edge on your competition, reading good poker books (notice the plural) is essential. You've already started with this one, so that's a great first step. Hopefully this isn't the first poker book you have read, and it should not be the last.

Poker books are abundant. They are also often repetitive. You will read a lot in this book that has no doubt been written several times before. Why then, you ask, should I read more books? Simple: repetition is one of the very best ways of learning. In your spare time, try this experiment. Write a paragraph of five to six sentences. Make them long and boring. Now, re-write that paragraph twenty times. After the twentieth time, aside from cramped fingers, you will have memorized that paragraph verbatim. The same goes with reading.

The more times you read and re-read a poker book, the more information you will absorb. Hopefully you will get to a point where you can almost repeat all of the concepts aloud. Then you can shelve the book and start on another one, going back to past books periodically as a reference to refresh your mind on certain concepts that might have faded over time.

Are you getting the picture that your poker education is a never-ending experience? It is. And reading is just a fraction of it. All of the things we outline in this chapter play a role in your poker education—even taking vacations away from the game. You can dedicate as much or as little time to your education as you wish, but remember this; you will get out of it what you put into it. We believe that if you are willing to put forth the effort, you will reap the rewards. Reading is not fun for everyone, but we promise that it will boost your poker skills exponentially if you do it correctly.

Read correctly? What on earth do you mean?

Poker books are to be studied rather than read. Most books you will read will contain such a vast number of concepts and theories that you will never grasp them all in your first time through the book. Thus, we feel the correct method is to read the text from cover to cover the first time. This will give you the feel for the book and assist your brain in understanding the task at hand. Once you can see the shore, you will know how far you have to swim to get there. After your first read-through, take a day or two to think about what you have read. Then go back and re-read each chapter several times in succession before advancing to the next. Not only will this technique ingrain the ideas in your mind, it will also build the foundation of knowledge you will need to advance to subsequent chapters. Most books build on themselves a chapter at a time. If you can fully comprehend everything in a chapter, you will be better prepared for concepts in the next.

Wow, you say. That's a lot of work! Sure it is. We never told you this was going to be easy. But if you want to use poker as a method of making money and enjoying a lifestyle you've only imagined until now, you are going to have to make an effort. Otherwise, these dreams will never come true.

Okay, so you are ready to read. Now the dilemma is book selection. There are so many out there! Where do I start? Your authors have read just about every poker book published. Many are good, several are great, many are poor, and some are just downright awful. In Appendix B, we list recommended books for aspiring poker players. Regardless of your game, with effort and hard work, these books will help you achieve the results you desire.

Now, there are other reading materials available to help you with your game. Back in the late 1970s, these items weren't available. But with today's technology, there is a wealth of poker knowledge available to you if you know where to find it. And the best part is, most of it is free!

On the Internet, there are several websites that host discussion forums. One in particular, www.twoplustwo.com, is one of the most widely read forums of its kind. Hosted by David Sklansky and Mason Malmuth, this site is broken down into multiple forums in order to streamline the discussions. It is also moderated to keep out junk posters and spam. The forums are updated by the minute, and they're free of charge.

If you are a user of Internet newsgroups, you will want to subscribe (again for free) to rec.gambling.poker. With literally hundreds of posts a day, this newsgroup is the cornerstone of online poker discussion. Granted, it is unmoderated, so you will have to wade through junk, but if you are patient, you will frequently find tips and valuable insight that will assist you in making your game as strong as it can be. Occasionally, a professional will post a useful tip.

Card Player Magazine has been around for years, and continues to be one of the most valuable sources for current poker information. With a fantastic selection of writers and topics, as well as tournament coverage and schedules, a subscription to *Card Player Magazine* is well worth the money. And, if you are fortunate enough to live near a legal card room, you might find free issues of *Card Player Magazine* distributed to patrons.

Several pros, like Mike Caro, Phil Hellmuth, David Sklansky and Howard Lederer, have developed instructional videos. If you are not much of a reader, these might be just the thing to jump-start your poker learning experience. Often these videos can be found used on eBay (www.ebay.com).

Keeping Accurate Records

In *Killer Poker*, John Vorhaus writes, "No poker player can even start to call himself serious-minded unless he keeps track of his performance over time. If he fails to keep track, it's not laziness, it's denial and fear."[34] The fact is, if you do not keep track of your earnings and other statistics, you have no way of accurately measuring your success. The mind tends to fool us, most likely as a defense mechanism, into thinking we are performing better than we are. Sure, keeping track of your wins and losses will be painful at times, but not doing so is being dishonest with yourself, and that can only hurt your game in the long run.

Keeping records is not only about knowing how much you have won or lost, or what your hourly win-rate is. It is about finding holes in your game and plugging them fast. The more extensive your records are, the more you will learn about your game. However, we know that keeping highly

---

34. John Vorhaus, *Killer Poker*, p. 205.

detailed records is tedious and often boring to some, so we recommend you keep track of at least the following:

1. Date

2. Location

3. Time In

4. Time Out

5. Total time played

6. Win/Loss

We advise you to keep a paper record of every session with those six items (as well as any other things you care to add). Then record that data into a spreadsheet or poker record-keeping software (we recommend some in Appendix B). Why keep paper records? First, it is always good to have a back-up in hardcopy in case your electronic data is lost or corrupted. Second, the IRS requires a written record if you are claiming your poker winnings as income (which, by the way, we believe you should).

From this data, you will be able to determine things like where you play the best, what games are most profitable for you, what days and times tend to provide the greatest return, and what limits are your best. You can determine what to avoid then, and focus on where you are making the most money. You can also determine what needs work.

If you are an online player, there are several software packages available to you that you can use to import hand histories. The software takes those hand histories and creates a virtually unlimited number of reports and interesting and valuable statistics on you and your play, plus that of your opponents. Many report this software to be extremely valuable and well worth the price.

Keeping poker records, once you begin, can be addicting. It is exciting to track your progress and earnings from month to month and year to year. If you can be honest with yourself and face your results with an open mind geared toward improving, you will soon find that accurate record keeping is an essential tool in every serious poker player's toolbox.

Keeping a Poker Journal

Unlike cold, hard statistics, a poker journal is a record of your feelings, thoughts and lessons learned. Think of it as a scrapbook of your poker education (which, as we discussed earlier, is a never-ending journey). The main purpose of keeping a poker journal is simple; it keeps your mind on the game when you are away from the table.

Also unlike your poker statistics, you are not confined to recording certain data in a poker journal. You might write something like, "The bankroll took a big hit last night in a brutal $2/$5 blind NL game when I flopped bottom set and lost to runner-runner flush by some moron who called to the river with no odds!" (It is okay to tell bad beat stories to yourself in your poker journal if it relieves some tension.) You might also write something philosophical like, "I've begun re-raising with QJs to add a little deception to my game. Being a normally very tight player, this seems to enhance my image a little, and I believe that making these kinds of raises at the right times causes my opponents to give me credit for a larger hand." You can also say something like, "Well, I made another $300 last night, bringing the bankroll up to almost $4,000. My win rate is pushing $14/hr., and I'm really feeling great about my game right now!"

Anything you feel like recording in your poker journal is fine, as long as it is related to your game in some way. We believe that the more you think about your game—and you can't write about the game without thinking about it—the stronger it will become. Remaining focused on your game, even when you are not playing, is a sign of a strong player.

Do not feel obligated to write every day or even every other day, but do try to make an effort at regular journal entries. We know some of you really enjoy writing (we sure do), but an equal number of you dread the thought. Although you might loathe the idea of putting pen to paper (or fingers to keys), we urge you to at least give it a shot. Try this: write just one sentence a day relating to your game. That's all. One sentence to capsulize your thoughts at that moment will be sufficient to create your journal. We'll bet you will soon begin writing more each time you open your journal once you get into the habit.

Every few months, go back and read what you've written. You might be surprised to see how much you have learned. Writing down your thoughts is an excellent way to gauge your progress—not by the numbers, but by your thinking. You will notice that you've advanced your mindset with each passing week, learning more and more. In fact, you might even laugh at your own naiveté upon reading your thoughts from just twelve months earlier.

This journal is for you, not for anyone else. The main purpose is your own poker growth. Recording the way you think about the game, the way you react to situations at the table, the emotions you go through and the constant battle for understanding is just one more way of managing your game. In time these thoughts and feelings will become automatic, and you will look forward to writing them down. Get in the habit of doing so. You'll be glad you did.

Maintaining a Proper Bankroll

Being prepared is essential. Not only should you have knowledge of proper play and strategy, but your mental and physical states must be in tune to your goals as well. Yet there is still one more thing to consider when playing poker: your bankroll.

A proper bankroll should be money set aside from your day-to-day financial considerations. This money is to be used for poker only, not to pay the bills or to buy a new entertainment center. The money you make from playing should be used to build this bankroll, with the goal to move up in limits when your bankroll allows. Have you ever wondered how some players in the card room are playing $50/$100 no-limit Hold'em while you're sitting at the $1/$2 no-limit table? Many are wealthy, but most have built their way up from the smaller games by supplementing their bankrolls with wins. You can do the same.

So, how much do you need? While there is no set guideline on this topic, we would like to recommend *at least* 20 buy-ins be in your bankroll. This is not the amount you will be taking to the card room whenever you play. This is your entire bankroll that you will be playing out of. This is the money behind the money you've got on the table. Let's look at some examples.

You like to play the $2/$3 blind, $100 fixed buy-in game in Southern California. You will need at least $2,000 in your bankroll to play that game on a regular basis. We say *regular basis* for a reason. If you plan on making this your usual game, you will need at least this much money to absorb the fluctuations you will undoubtedly face in the course of play. If you have a big loss one day, it's no problem, as your bankroll can sustain those temporary setbacks. You can still play the next day.

Keep in mind, there's nothing wrong with "taking a shot" and playing a little higher than your bankroll would normally permit every so often. After a nice win one afternoon, you've got the urge to jump into the $300 buy-in game with $2 and $5 blinds. Go ahead and try it out. Just be aware that your current bankroll isn't nearly enough to support regular play in this game. In fact, for this game, you would like to have $6,000 in reserves if you plan on making it your regular game.

As you move up, you might even try the $5/$10 blind, $500 buy-in game. For this game, you will need a bankroll of $10,000. Just multiply the maximum buy-in by twenty and you will arrive at your minimum bankroll requirement.

Now, how much do you bring to the card room? You certainly don't want to bring your entire bankroll with you. As a general rule, bringing five buy-ins with you should be enough. And don't think that you will be putting all of this in play if things go badly. You are bringing enough money with you to play comfortably in this game. If you lose your first buy-in, and then immediately lose your second and are now half-way into your third, you might want to consider packing it in for the day. You still have plenty of bankroll behind you, and today just doesn't seem to be your day to make money. That's what a bankroll is for; to allow you to come back the next day and the next, fresh and ready to play with re-buys in your pocket.

Does this amount sound excessive? It shouldn't. In fact, our guideline of twenty buy-ins is a minimum. The more ammunition you have, the better prepared you will be for the war. You might lose a few battles along the way, but in the end, you will prevail because you were prepared for anything. Make your bankroll a priority, and be firm with yourself when it comes to maintaining it. Don't spend it. If you find yourself in a financial crunch, don't play poker for a while. Straighten yourself out before going to the tables, and when you do play, play prepared.

Taking Vacations

So you've played six consecutive days without booking a win, and you are dreading the trip to the card room planned for this evening. So why not skip a night? In fact, why not take three days off; or a week; or even longer?

We're big advocates of getting away from the game from time to time to refresh and regroup. If you are starting to feel as used and abused as hotel laundry, and you can't seem to book a win no matter wshat you do, *stop playing for a while!* Sure, the game is great and yeah, maybe you are the best player in it, but right now you're in no shape to play cards. Starting out with a defeatist attitude and almost expecting one more night of bad cards and bad beats is not a good idea. How can you possibly expect to turn your slump around with that kind of mindset? You are just begging for another night of abuse, and more often than not, you will get it.

Regardless of how good you think you are playing now, chances are that an extended losing streak has a lot to do with your game. But you can't see it, so how can that be? Ah, herein lies the writer's dilemma; he doesn't notice his own mistakes. This is why writers do not edit their own books. A fresh pair of eyes is the key. The same applies to poker. You need a fresh pair of eyes to look at your game. You've probably developed a series of small leaks in your quest to end your misery, but you are so blinded by your recent losses that you can't see the little things you are doing wrong. Now those little things are adding up, and it is only going to get worse. Get away from the game—*fast!*

We do not care what you do or where you go, but it is best to be in no close proximity to a card room. Take a week and read a book. Take a trip. Take a nap. Whatever. Just get away from the game for a while and think about something else. Remember when we said earlier that life is a lot more than just poker? Well, this is one of those times when you need to step back into "real life." Shift your concentration away from the game for a while. You will be surprised to find you are looking at the game in a different light when you return to it, and you might start to see things you've never seen before. All of this can only improve your game—not to mention your quality of life.

Final Thoughts

As you can see, there is so much more to poker than the play of cards and the splash of chips. Managing your game is an integral part of your poker success. So often, your actions away from the table have a huge impact on your performance while in the game. The extra effort you exert to improve your game—in ways others most players never even consider—will go a long way toward making you the best player you can be. If you persist in your efforts, you can achieve a level of skill that will afford you the spoils of the game.

And if all that wasn't enough incentive to work on your game away from the table, remember this: making a concentrated effort to manage your game when you are not playing will build your confidence to heights you might never have thought possible. This confidence, when taken into battle, is extremely difficult for your weak opponents to overcome. Sitting down at the table knowing you *are* probably the most skilled in that group is possibly the biggest weapon of all. Not only will your skill become a chip magnet, it will also make you appear poised, determined, and ready for anything. When you exude confidence, most players will sense that you are not one to be messed with. Imagine what you can do with that in a no-limit game!

Chapter 12

Conclusion

C ongratulations! You've made it to the final chapter. We hope it has been an enjoyable and educational experience for you. We've covered many topics of this fascinating game, and we believe that the lessons provided in the pages you have read will set you on your path to becoming a more successful player.

In closing, we'd like to reiterate something we mentioned in Chapter 11 about reading books. Like any poker book, we believe this one is one to be studied several times over, not just read once. Your poker study never ends. You will learn something new every time you play the game or pick up a book. Even if you think you've taken everything out of this book that you can, go back sometime in the future and read it again. It's always wise to stay fresh and remind yourself of the basics. Picking up this book every once in a while is a great way to do just that.

As you've learned, becoming a successful no-limit hold'em player requires a great deal of skill. You must be proficient at reading hands and opponents. You must know what types of opponents you're facing and how they might react to certain situations depending upon their tendencies, their cards and the size of their stacks. You must acquire a solid working knowledge of pot odds (including implied odds) as well as the odds of your hand improving. You must understand the reasons why you bet certain amounts in certain situations, and what those bets mean when your opponent makes them. You must understand what hands to play, how to play them, and most importantly, the value of position and how it affects your play. You must grasp all of the playing strategies on every round of betting, and you must know when to push a big hand or let one go. You need to know when a draw is profitable and when it is best to fold. Being able to recognize the effects of stack-size, blind-size and opponent types is also essential. Finally, managing your game and your mind come into play, and they might just be your keys to success.

Yes, we have covered a lot of ground. It's now up to you to decide what to do with this knowledge. We hope that you take it to the tables and use it to make the price of this book insignificant. But before you do that, you'll need to have a plan.

We suggest starting out small. Play the lowest limit game you can find. Most card rooms offer small buy-in and small blind games. If you're an Internet player, you can even find blinds as low as 1¢/2¢. The play at these very small games will be different than what you will face in a "normal" game ($1/$2 blinds and higher), but you will get a feel for the game, the betting, and how to react to certain types of opponents. As you become familiar with the game and more comfortable with your play, you can start thinking about the larger games. But don't jump into them just yet. Make sure you are playing a tight, solid, aggressive game. You will need to be even more careful in the bigger games, so make sure you've got the bankroll to sustain any short-term losses you might incur. Move up in limits slowly as you progress in your game and build your bankroll. There is no hurry. The games will be there tomorrow and the next day and the next. Be patient with yourself. Manage your mind and your game. No-limit hold'em can be quite frustrating, especially during a long run of bad cards and bad beats. Don't let these things get you down. They are simply temporary setbacks and a part of the game for everyone. The best players—and we mean the *very best* players—are the ones who can handle the swings better than anyone else. Keeping a level head is perhaps your greatest and most effective weapon.

And hey, have some fun! When the game no longer provides enjoyment for you, it's time to quit. The more you enjoy yourself, the better your mind will perform and the better you will play. This is a great time to be a poker player, and there is a great deal of money to be made if you know how to make it. We hope we have provided you with a direct path to that money. You're standing at the start of a great adventure. You have the tools and the knowledge necessary to win. What you do now is up to you. Good luck, and play well!

Quiz

I t's impossible for one quiz to cover all of the situations you will be faced with when playing no-limit hold'em. In this quiz we present to you some of the more common decisions you will be faced with, and what we would do in these situations. For all of the problems in the quiz, assume that you are playing in a $100 fixed buy-in no-limit hold'em game with blinds of $2/$3. You may ignore the rake for purposes of answering these questions. For all of the questions in this section, assume that you have an average stack for your game ($150).

Hand Selection (I)

Questions:

For each question, state what you would do (a) if first to act, (b) in middle position, (c) on the button, and (d) in the small blind.

1.   You hold A♠A♥ and *everyone* folds to you.

2.   You hold 7♠7♣ and *everyone* folds to you.

3.   You hold T♦3♦ and *everyone* folds to you.

4.   You hold T♦3♦ and *everyone* limps before you. *Note: Only answer (b), (c), and (d) for this problem.*

5.   You hold K♦J♣ and two players have limped in front of you. *Note: Only answer (b), (c), and (d) for this problem.*

Answers:

1.   (a) (b) (c) and (d). Raise. It is much better to win a small pot than to lose a big pot. We would raise to $12 (presumed standard raise). If you don't raise, what will you

do when the flop comes 4♣4♥Q♦? If you check, would you bet if the turn were the 4♠? The big blind, holding 7♠4♦, is waiting for you to act.

2. (a) We did not give you enough information to answer this question. Is the game passive? If so, a raise might be correct. Is the game loose-aggressive? Then you should fold. Give yourself credit no matter how you answered (a). (b) Either calling or raising is correct—see the answer to part (a). (c) and (d) Raise. Your pair is probably the best hand.

3. (a) (b) (c) (d) Fold. You have a trash hand. If you chop blinds, offer to do so in (d). Why would you voluntarily put money in the pot with trash?

4. (b) Fold. You still have a trash hand. What do you do if the flop comes 7♦5♦2♦? Mr. Murphy guarantees that if you bet, one of your opponents will hold J♦4♦, while if you check your diamond flush is high (until a fourth diamond comes on the turn or river). And if you don't get a perfect flop, you will have wasted $3 calling with a trash hand. Fold and move on. (c) Fold. Yes, you're getting great odds for your money but you have a junk hand. Unless the flop comes TT3 (or a close variation thereof), you're always going to be in doubt. (d) Call, but ever so reluctantly. You have the correct pot odds to call, but hope for a flop containing two tens or two threes, because there's not much else you want to see from first position.

5. (b) Fold. You have a trap hand. If the flop comes Jxx, do you really want to bet when invariably someone holds AJ to your KJ? Why not solve the problem by waiting for a better hand? Also, you cannot stand a raise and half the field is yet to act. (c) Raise. Your hand is likely the best hand at the table. If you're called, you

will have position on the later betting rounds. If you're re-raised, you will have to play the player but we would be inclined to fold. (d) Call. You're going to be out of position in the remaining betting rounds, but you are certainly getting the right price to see the flop.

Hand Selection (II)

Questions:

6. You hold Q♠Q♣ on the button. The under-the-gun player raises to $12. The next player re-raises to $25. The next player calls. The next player, a new player who had posted his $3 blind, moves all-in for $100. Everyone folds to you. What do you do?

7. You hold Q♠Q♣ on the button. The under-the-gun player raises to $12. Everyone folds to you. What do you do?

8. The under the gun player raises to $6, and everyone calls to you, the big blind. You look down at 7♣2♠. What do you do?

9. You are under the gun and hold A♣K♣ and raise to $12. A middle position player that you know is a maniac re-raises to $25. The big blind, a solid player, thinks for about a minute before calling. Everyone else folds. It's your turn to act. What do you do?

10. You are in middle position with A♠Q♠, and after everyone folds to you, you raise to $12. The button calls and the small blind, Tight Ted, the tightest player in your cardroom, re-raises to $25. The big blind folds and it's your turn to act. What do you do?

Answers:

6. You have three opponents (don't forget the player that just called). All are representing good hands. Not

knowing anything about your opponents, you're in a coin-toss situation *at best* (surely someone holds AK). At worst, you're a huge underdog. The worst-case scenario is much likelier than the best-case scenario (which isn't that great of a situation). Folding is the best play.

7. Re-raise or fold, depending on the player. If you don't know the player, or the player was loose, you should re-raise. If the player is tight, you should fold. Queens are a good hand, but aces and kings are better (and if your opponent holds AK, you're in a coin-toss situation).

8. Fold. You earn money playing poker by (1) winning hands and (2) not losing money on hands. Let's assume you call, and the flop comes 7♥4♥3♦. You have top pair, lousy kicker. Do you want to bet that hand? Think about how many flops you want to see holding 72o. Folding will save you $3, money that's in your stack and part of your win (or lessening your loss).

9. You probably have the best hand. What does the maniac hold? Any two cards, of course. What does the solid player hold? He either has a very good hand (e.g. AA) or he has a hand where he wants you to call so that he gets the right odds to be in the pot—say a medium pair. The only hands that you don't want to see from the solid player are AA and KK. If the solid player holds QQ (or any smaller pair), you're in a coin-toss situation. If he holds a small pair or suited connectors he can't call you. Your goal is to get heads-up against the maniac. Thus, you should re-raise, probably moving all-in.

10. Fold. The tightest player is raising and you hold AQ. Every so often, you will be in a coin-toss situation; how-

ever, you're probably trailing Ted. And nothing prevents the button from holding a good hand, too!

The Flop

Questions:

11. You hold 5♦4♦ in the big blind. Four players limp to you (the small blind folds), so you get to see the flop for free. The flop comes A♦8♦3♦ giving you the flush. You must act first on the flop. What is your action?

12. You hold Q♦Q♥ in the cut-off seat. There are two limpers to you, you raise to $20, and only one of the limpers calls you (everyone else folds). The flop doesn't appear threatening: 7♥7♣3♠. However, to your surprise, the pre-flop limper bets $30 (he has you out-chipped). It's your turn to act; what is your action?

13. Assume the same information as in question 12 *except* the pre-flop limper checks (he has you out-chipped). What is your action?

14. You hold T♠9♠ in the cut-off seat. Four players limp to you pre-flop and you elect to raise to $20. The big blind and the four limpers *all* call you (it's a loose game). The flop comes Q♠T♦8♠ giving you a flush draw, an inside straight draw, a one-card straight flush draw, and middle pair. The big blind bets $5. The next two players call. The next player folds. The next player thinks for about thirty seconds and moves all-in for a total of $40. The three other players left in the hand all have similar stacks to your own. What is your action?

15. You are in the small blind with 5♠5♣. Four players limp, you elect to call, but the big blind raises to $7. All of the limpers call, so you call the $4 raise. The flop

looks good for you: T♦T♥5♥, giving you fives full of tens. You're first to act. What is your action?

Answers:

11. Bet around the size of the pot. You probably have the best hand until another diamond falls. Given the rank of your flush, winning a small pot looks better than losing a big pot.

12. What does your opponent hold? Is he bluffing? Hands like this one are why some of us get grey hair! If our opponent has AA, KK, 7x, or 33, you're behind and in serious trouble. If he holds anything else (except the other two queens), you're ahead, and in great shape. If your opponent is tight and solid, a fold is probably correct; he likely has one of the hands that beats you. If you were up against anyone else, you should raise (to $80). The most likely hand for your opponent is an overpair to the board but an underpair to your hand.

13. Bet $30. We're not big fans of slow-playing hands like this. Assume your opponent holds AQ and you check. What do you do when an ace falls on the turn?

14. Call (if you know all of your opponents would call a raise, you should raise). This is a great flop for your hand. You might already have the best hand. If you don't, you have a lot of outs to make the best hand. You want your opponents to call because you are still drawing.

15. Check. If one of your opponents holds T♣5♦, it's just not your day. This is the kind of hand to slow-play.

The Turn

Questions:

16. You hold 9♠8♠ and raise to $12 from the cut-off position pre-flop. Only the blinds call you. The flop comes 7♠6♠2♣ giving you an open-ended straight flush draw. The small blind's eyes go wide when he sees the flop. He bets $35, the big blind folds, and you elect to call. The turn is the Q♦. The small blind frowns when that card comes out and then thinks for about thirty seconds. He then bets $30 and you must act. What do you do?

17. Assume the same situation as in question 16 except that the small blind moves all-in on the turn (he has you outchipped). What is your action?

18. You hold 3♠2♦ in the big blind. Pre-flop, four players and the small blind limp and you check your option. The flop is A♠K♠Q♣ and you mentally get ready to fold—except everyone checks. The turn is the 4♥, giving you a draw to a wheel. The small blind bets $10. What is your action?

19. You hold A♥K♥ on the button. Pre-flop, two players limp into the hand and you raise to $20. Both of the limpers call your raise (everyone else folds). The flop comes J♠9♣4♥. Both limpers check and you decide to bet $35. Only the first limper calls. The turn is the T♥ giving you a flush draw, an inside straight draw, and two overcards. Your opponent checks. What is your action? Your opponent also started the hand with $150.

20. You hold 4♠4♣ in early position. You limp pre-flop, as does the cutoff; however, the button raises to $20. You and the cutoff both call. The flop comes J♠9♣4♥ giv-

ing you bottom set. You and the cutoff both check. The button bets $35 and you call while the cutoff folds. The turn is the T♥. You must act first. What is your action? If you check, and your opponent bets $40, what would your action then be? Your opponent also started the hand with $150.

Answers:

16. Let's first determine the pot odds. There's $136 in the pot, and it will cost you $30 to call. You have fifteen outs (nine spades, three tens, and three fives). There are 46 unknown cards, giving you a 15/46 chance of hitting a winning hand (32.6%), or pot odds of about 3 to 1. The pot is laying you 4.5 to 1. A call is clear.

17. You have the same chance of making your hand; however, the cost to call your opponent's bet will be more. You started the hand with $150, and you have already put $47 into the pot. Thus, your opponent's bet is effectively $103. That means there's effectively $209 in the pot and the pot is laying you just over 2 to 1. You no longer have the correct pot odds to call. A fold is the right choice.

18. Fold. There are several players left to act. Your hand is atrocious. You could have *no* outs if someone is holding JT. Why put any money into this pot?

19. What does your opponent hold to call you on the flop? Perhaps he has QT and flopped a straight draw. Perhaps he has AJ or A9 and flopped a pair. He could have 99 or 44 and have flopped a set (JJ is unlikely because he probably would have re-raised pre-flop). He could have a middle pair (TT) and believe you missed the flop and were bluffing. There's $130 in the pot and you have $95 left. If you bet, you're pretty much forced to bet all-in. What is the chance your opponent

would fold top pair to your all-in bet? There's no chance he would fold a set. Unless you have a clear read that your opponent has a set, you should move all-in here. Even if he has the set, you have a number of outs (non-pairing heart and a queen). Similarly, you have more outs if he calls with top pair. It's entirely possible that he will fold top pair (putting you on a big hand).

20. You have trapped your opponent. Given that the board is now threatening you to some degree (if your opponent has QJ, he now has a straight draw), you should move all-in now.

The River

Questions:

21. You are in the big blind with 7♥2♣. Five other players limp pre-flop (the small blind folds). The flop comes Q♣J♣T♣. Everyone checks the flop. The turn is the 5♣, giving you the smallest possible flush. Again, everyone checks. The river is the 5♦. You must act first. What is your action?

22. You hold K♦Q♦ in the cutoff seat. Pre-flop, a maniac raises to $13, with the player to your right, you, and the button all calling. The flop is K♥Q♣6♦ giving you top two pair and a backdoor flush draw. The maniac bets $20 on the flop. The player to your right folds, you call, as does the button. The turn is the 2♠. The maniac bets $30, with you and the button calling. The river is the A♠, and the maniac moves all-in for $200! With your peripheral vision, you steal a glance at the button. Unfortunately, there's nary a sign of a tell from him (you have previously classified him as a solid play-

er), so you're on your own. Do you call all-in for your last $100 or do you fold? The button has $120 left.

23. You are on the button with Q♣J♣. Pre-flop, two play-ers limp, you raise to $13 and get a call from the big blind and one of the limpers. You flop a straight-flush draw (the flop is T♣9♣3♠). The other players check the flop and you bet $30. Only the big blind calls. The turn is the unhelpful 2♥. The big blind checks, and you bet $40. The big blind thinks for about thirty seconds and calls. The river is the A♦. (a) Assume the big blind moves all-in for $60. Do you call? (b) If the big blind checks (he has $60 left), what is your action?

24. You hold T♥T♠ in the big blind. An aggressive, some-what loose middle position player raises pre-flop to $12 and you are the lone caller. The flop comes Q♥8♠4♣. You check, and the aggressive player bets $15, which you call. The turn is the 4♠. You elect to check, and the aggressive player again bets $15. You call that bet, too. The river is the 3♥. What is your bet-ting strategy for the river?

25. You hold 7♠6♠ in the big blind. Six players (including the small blind) limp, and you see the flop for free. You do a double take when you see the flop: 8♠5♠4♠. You've flopped a straight flush! The small blind checks the flop, and you check also. You are somewhat disap-pointed when everyone else checks behind you. The turn is the A♣, giving you the stone-cold nuts. The small blind checks the turn, and you decide to check one more time as well. However, the next player bets $20. Everyone folds to the small blind who calls. You also call. The river is the K♠. The small blind bets $30 (he has *at least* $300 left in his stack). You remember that your other opponent has about the same stack

size as you. You have $127 left in your stack. What action do you take on the river?

Answers:

21. Your hand is beat by any club, or by a full house. If everyone checks and you win the pot, be thankful. Check, and fold to any bet.

22. This hand comes from actual play (one of the authors was the button). First, if you are heads-up with a maniac, slow playing this hand is correct. But there's another player in this hand—a solid player who must have *something* to still be in the hand. Possible hands include a draw, a set, or two pair. Given that, we strongly believe that the cutoff should have raised all-in on the turn (raising all-in on the flop would be a close second choice) to knock out the button. Now, to the actual conditions of the problem. First, there's no way to tell what the maniac has. Second, your hand is probably not the best hand outstanding. Why did the solid player continue on the hand? Once he calls the turn, he must have one of the hands mentioned above (draw, set, or two pair). You can beat the latter (or tie if he also has KQ) but lose to a set. What kind of draw might he hold? The most likely is JTs giving him a straight draw and a backdoor flush draw on the flop. If he holds that hand, he has a clear call on the flop and turn based on pot odds (and implied odds). His JTs is now the best hand and if you call you're going to lose. The actual hands held were A♣A♦ by the maniac and J♥T♥ by the button. The actual cutoff did fold.

23. (a) You can't bluff the big blind out of the hand after he moves his chips in. You can't beat a pair of deuces. A fold is clear. (b) We would bet $60. If you check, you're likely going to lose the hand. If you bet, continuing to

represent a big hand, your bluff will work enough of the time to make it worthwhile. When the big blind asks, let him know you held AT.

24. You should make a half-pot size bet on the river. You may have the best hand—your somewhat loose opponent could be on AKs, for example. You may be trailing—he could hold AQs. More times than not you will be ahead, though. And if you bet, two of the three things that can happen are good. If your opponent comes over the top, you have a tough decision (this is the lone reason in support of check-calling). You should base your action on the history of the opponent. If you knew nothing about him, you should be inclined to call (but just barely).

25. Obviously, you are going to win this hand. The question is how do you extract the most money from your opponents. Suppose you just call the small blind. Will the other player left in the hand call? If he would, that action is worth $30 to you. Now assume you were to raise to $65. What would the two other players left in the hand do? Most likely, the other player would fold. If the small blind would call, then that choice is worth $35 to you. Our inclination would be to make a small raise (to $65 or $70). You hope to induce a re-raise (possible if the small blind holds, for example, A♠8♣). It's probable that the other player flopped a flush and is unlikely to call any bet. Of course, you will be happy if either player re-raises, too!

An Eight-hour No-limit Hold'em Session

This appendix lists the hands that were played during an eight-hour session of $100 fixed buy-in no-limit hold'em at the Bicycle Casino in Bell Gardens, California in late November 2004. The opposition was quite typical: a couple of good players, a couple of horrible players, and some average players. The game started four-handed but quickly filled to nine-handed after the first fifteen minutes. The blinds were $2/$3.

1. 87o (button). Raise to $10; win pot; tip 50¢. Stack: $104.

2. 52o. Fold. Stack: $104.

3. 94o (bb). sb calls. Flop KQJ. Check, check. Turn 2; all check. River 4. All check. Win $5. Stack: $109.

4. 32o (sb). Button raises to 10; fold. Stack: $107.

5. 33. Raise to $12, win pot; tip 50¢. Stack: $111.

6. 92o. Fold. Stack: $111.

7. 72o. Fold. Stack: $111.

8. 52o. Fold. Stack: $111.

9. AKs (bb). Good middle-position player raises to $12. I re-raise to $30. He moves all-in, I call. He holds 88. The flop has an 8 and I lose. Stack: $24. I rebuy $100 in chips. Adjusted stack: $124.

10. T3o (sb). Fold. Stack: $124.

11. 92o. Fold. Stack: $124.

12. T7s. Fold. Stack: $124.

13. 43o. Fold. Stack: $124.

14. JTo. Fold. Stack: $124.

15. J7s (bb). Fold to pre-flop raise to $10. Stack: $121.

16. A6o (sb). Fold to pre-flop raise to $15. Stack: $119.

17. 85o (button). Fold. Stack: $119.

18. T5o. Fold. Stack: $119.

19. K8o. Fold. Stack: $119.

20. 97o. Fold. Stack: $119.

21. KTs. Fold. Stack: $119. Had I played this hand to the end I would have won the pot; the turn and river were tens.

22. ATo. Fold. Stack: $119.

23. Q3o. Fold. Stack: $119.

24. 82o (bb). Fold to pre-flop raise to $10. Stack: $116.

25. AKo (sb). Pre-flop raise to $6 with two callers. I re-raise to $30 and win the pot. Stack: $126.

26. 64o (button). Fold. Stack: $126.

27. 84o. Fold. Stack: $126.

28. AKo. Pre-flop raise to $10. I re-raise to $35 and am called. The flop is 888. Checked. Turn is a 2. Checked. River is a 4. Checked. My AK is good (other player held ATo) and I win $35 ($3 is dropped for the rake, $1 is the jackpot drop, and I tipped $1). My opponent was a good player who could easily have held a pair or an 8. Stack: $161.

29. 53o. Fold. Stack: $161.

30. KK (UTG). I raise to $15 and am called by a player I have never played against. The flop is J84 rainbow. I bet $25 and am called. The turn is another 4 (completing the rainbow). I bet $100 and my opponent calls all-in. We never see his hand as the river is a king giving me the nut full house. I net $100 on this hand. Stack: $261 (I am now up $61 for the day).

31. QTo (bb). There is a pre-flop raise to $6 with two callers and I call. The flop is A83. Checked. The turn is a T. Checked. The river is a 3. Checked. My QT is good and I net $20. There is more to this hand. I have a reputation for being tight and the raiser was the same person who held 88 against my AK. I wanted him to see my QT and that I would call from the big blind with weaker hands – I wanted him to see my hand and though I felt I had the best hand deliberately checked. Stack: $281.

32. 52o (sb). Fold. Stack: $279.

33. 64o (button). Fold. Stack: $279.

34. 53o. Fold. Stack: $279.

35. A9s. Fold. Stack: $279.

36. 42o. Fold. Stack: $279.

37. Q4o (bb). Fold to pre-flop raise to $6. Stack: $276.

38. ATo (sb). Call. *Family pot* (everyone is in). Flop is T52. I bet $18 and take the pot. My net win is $19. Stack: $295.

39. 84o (button). Fold. Stack: $295.

40. 66. Fold to pre-flop raise to $18. Stack: $295.

41. J5o. Fold. Stack: $295.

42. K8s. Fold. Stack: $295.

43. T7o. Fold. Stack: $295.

44. Q6s. Fold. Stack: $295.

45. 98s. Post the blinds ($5). Fold to pre-flop raise to $10. I would have flopped two pair and have been in third place as both 99 and 88 were out! Stack: $290.

46. Q2o. Fold. Stack: $290.

47. T2o. Fold. Stack: $290.

48. JTo. Fold. Stack: $290.

49. 85o. Fold. Stack: $290.

50. T6o (bb). Fold to pre-flop raise to $18. Stack: $287.

51. T3o (sb). Fold to pre-flop raise to $6. Stack: $285.

52. 87o. Fold. Stack: $285.

53. QTo. Fold (there was a pre-flop raise to $18). Stack: $285.

54. AQo. Call (four see flop). Flop is T99. Bet of $15 and raise to $30 in front of me. Fold. Stack: $282.

55. J9o. Fold. Stack: $282.

56. K6o (bb). Fold to pre-flop raise to $13. Stack: $279.

57. Q4o (sb). Call, then fold to bb's raise to $20. Stack: $276.

58. 84o (button). Fold. Stack: $276.

59. 64o. Fold. Stack: $276.

60. K9o. Fold. Stack: $276.

61. K8s. Fold. Stack: $276.

62. KJo. Fold. I would have flopped a straight. Stack: $276.

63. 72o. Fold. Stack: $276.

64. Q4s (bb). Four call and I check. The flop is AK8. The sb bets $10 and I fold. Stack: $273.

65. 77 (sb). I call a pre-flop raise to $10 (two other callers). The flop is AAK. I fold to the bet of $30. Stack: $263.

66. T6s (button). Fold. Stack: $263.

67. J7o. Fold. Stack: $263.

68. Q3o. Fold. Stack: $263.

69. AJo. Fold to pre-flop raise to $15. Stack: $263.

70. K5o. Fold. Stack: $263.

71. T3o. Fold. Stack: $263.

72. 76o (bb). The action goes: limp, raise to $6, with 3 callers. I call. The original limper re-raises to $30 and I fold (when it gets back to me). Stack: $257.

73. 42o (sb). Fold. Stack: $255.

74. T4o. Fold (pre-flop raises to $15 and $40). Stack: $255.

75. 95o. Fold. Stack: $255.

76. K5o. Fold. Stack: $255.

77. QQ. There is a raise to $6, I re-raise to $20, the next player calls. The sb re-raises to $80. He is a good player and I feel I am beat so I fold. He has KK (the other player holds 88). Stack: $235.

78. A2o. Fold. Stack: $235.

79. 42o. Fold. Stack: $235.

80. K5o (bb). Fold to pre-flop raise to $8. Stack: $232.

81. J2o (sb). Fold, even with five callers. Stack: $230.

82. 75o (button). Fold. Stack: $230.

83. T4s. Fold. Stack: $230.

84. 32o. Fold. Stack: $230.

85. 86o. Fold. Stack: $230.

86. KK. I raise to $15, one player calls. On Q83 flop I bet $25 and win the pot. I win $18. Stack: $248.

87. 43o. Fold. Stack: $248.

88. 42o. Fold. Stack: $248.

89. 65o (bb). I call the raise to $6. Seven see a flop of QQ8 (I fold). Stack: $242.

90. A2o (sb). I fold to pre-flop raise to $20. Stack: $240.

91. J7o. Fold. Stack: $240.

92. AQo. Two callers, I raise to $25 and win the pot and tip 50¢. Stack: $250.

93. 32o. Fold. Stack: $250.

94. AQo. I call (along with four others). The flop is 776. I fold to a $20 bet. Stack: $247.

95. J7o. Fold. Stack: $250.

96. Q9o (bb). Fold to pre-flop raise to $15. Stack: $247.

97. 43s (sb). I call, but the big blind raises to $13 and I then fold. Stack: $244.

98. 92s. Fold. Stack: $244.

99. K8o. Fold. Stack: $244.

100. T8s. Fold to pre-flop raise to $6. Stack: $244.

101. 74o. Fold. Stack: $244.

102. 53o (bb). Fold. Stack: $241.

103. K5o (sb). Fold. Stack: $239.

104. ATo (button). I fold to the raises (first to $6, then $28). Stack: $239.

105. 93o. Fold. Stack: $239.

106. KK. I re-raise from $15 to $45 and win the pot. Stack: $258.

107. 63o. Fold. Stack: $258.

108. 86o. Fold. Stack: $258.

109. 63o (bb). Fold to pre-flop raise to $10. Stack: $255.

110. Q4o (sb). Fold to pre-flop raise to $15. Stack: $253.

111. K6o. Fold. Stack: $253.

112. Q5o. Fold. Stack: $253.

113. QQ. Raise to $15, all fold. Stack: $260.

114. 63o. Fold. Stack: $260.

115. 32o (bb). Fold to pre-flop raise to $15. Stack: $257.

116. AJo (sb). Fold to pre-flop raise to $15. Stack: $255.

117. Q8o. Fold. Stack: $255

118. J6s. Fold. Stack: $255.

119. A2o. Fold to pre-flop raise to $22. Stack: $255.

120. T7o. Fold. Stack: $255.

121. 75s. Fold. Stack: $255.

122. 76o. Fold. Stack: $255.

123. 42s. Fold. Stack: $255.

124. KK (bb). I re-raise a pre-flop raise to $7 followed by a call to $23 and win the pot. Stack: $270.

125. A2s (sb). I call, along with four others. The flop is QTT. I fold (the flop bet is $20). Stack: $267.

126. J4o. Fold. Stack: $267.

127. J2s. Fold. Stack: $267.

128. 64o. Fold. Stack: $267.

129. A9o. Fold. Stack: $267.

130. K9s. Fold. Stack: $267.

131. JTs. Fold. Stack: $267.

132. QQ (bb). Three players call, I raise to $23 and take the pot. Stack: $277.

133. QTo (sb). I fold to pre-flop raise to $18. Stack: $275.

134. 98o. Fold. Stack: $275.

135. J8o. Fold. Stack: $275.

136. KQo. Fold. Stack: $275. During this time period our game had a calling station that would call any bet or raise. Given my position and the liveliness of the game, I felt no need to call or raise with this trap hand.

137. 43s. Fold. Stack: $275.

138. 82s. Fold. Stack: $275.

139. QJo (bb). Fold to pre-flop raise to $15. Stack: $272.

140. 98o (sb). Fold to pre-flop raise to $15. Stack: $270.

141. 74s. Fold. Stack: $270.

142. K2o. Fold. Stack: $270.

143. J2o. Fold. Stack: $270.

144. 75o. Fold. Stack: $270.

145. A2o. Fold. Stack: $270.

146. T3o. Fold. Stack: $270.

147. 97o (bb). I check, five see flop of KQ2. The bet is $20 and I fold. Stack: $267.

148. 83o (sb). Fold. Stack: $265.

149. J3o. Fold. Stack: $265.

150. T7o (UTG). Fold. Stack: $265.

151. JJ (bb). It is raised to $6 with two callers. I re-raise to $26 and win the pot. Stack: $284.

152. 99 (sb). I call, along with four others; the big blind raises to $69. Everyone folds. Stack: $281.

153. 54o. Fold. Stack: $281.

154. 84o. Fold. Stack: $281.

155. K3s. Fold. Stack: $281.

156. J9o. Fold. Stack: $281.

157. J6s. Fold. Stack: $281.

158. KJo (bb). I check and four see a flop of AdJd7d. I check and fold to the bet of $15 (he shows AJo). Stack: $278.

159. 53s (sb). I fold to the pre-flop raise to $6. Stack: $276.

160. 97s. I call, along with three others. The flop is KhQhTh (my suit is clubs). I fold to the bet of $16. Stack: $273.

161. K3o. Fold. Stack: $273.

162. 87o. Fold. Stack: $273.

163. 33. Call, with four others. Flop is A87. I fold to the flop bet of $17. Stack: $270.

164. 76o. Fold. Stack: $270.

165. 63o. Fold. Stack: $270.

166. 53o (bb). I fold to the pre-flop raise to $6. Stack: $267.

167. T5o (sb). I fold to the pre-flop raise to $20. Stack: $265.

168. 96o. Fold. Stack: $265.

169. K7s. Fold. Stack: $265.

170. K6o. Fold. Stack: $265.

171. 66. Call, with three others. Flop QQJ. All check. Turn: K. I fold to a bet of $15. Stack: $262.

172. TT (UTG). Raise to $15, win pot. Stack: $266.

173. QJo (bb). I call the raise to $6 with two others. Flop AJ4. I bet $10 and win the pot. Stack: $281.

174. 98o (sb). I fold to the pre-flop raise to $6. Stack: $279.

175. Q6s. Fold. Stack: $279.

176. J2o. Fold. Stack: $279.

177. A2o. Fold. Stack: $279.

178. J3o. Fold. Stack: $279.

179. 33 (bb). I call, four see flop of J93. I check, next player bets $15, I call with one other. Turn is an 8. All Check. River is a 2. I bet $50, next player raises to $100, next player folds. I push all-in, opponent calls and shows 98o. I win $225. Stack: $504.

180. K9s (sb). I call raise to $6. It's then re-raised to $30 with six callers! I elect to call. The flop is A97 rainbow. It's bet ($50) and raised ($101) in front of me and I fold. Stack: $474.

181. AQs (button). Everyone calls, I raise to $23 and take the pot. Stack: $497.

182. 96o. Fold. Stack: $497.

183. 74s. Fold. Stack: $497.

184. AQo. It's folded to me. I raise to $15. The player who lost to me with 98 re-raises all-in (he could have anything) $81. I put him on an ace, but have no idea how big. In retrospect I should fold – I'm not likely a favorite. However, I call. He holds AKo and nothing good happens from my point of view. Stack: $416.

185. 84o. Fold. Stack: $416.

186. JTo. Fold. Stack: $416.

187. J6o (bb). I fold to a pre-flop raise of $20. Stack: $413.

188. 65o (sb). Fold. Stack: $411.

189. 73o. Fold. Stack: $411.

190. K4o. Fold. Stack: $411.

191. K9o (bb). I fold to a pre-flop raise of $12. Stack: $408.

192. 83o (sb). Fold. Stack: $406.

193. 64o. Fold. Stack: $406.

194. A2s. I fold to a pre-flop raise to $40. Stack: $406.

195. 42o. Fold. Stack: $406.

196. K3o. Fold. Stack: $406.

197. 54s. Fold. Stack: $406.

198. 65o (bb). I check, with three others. Flop 932 rainbow. All check. Turn is a 6. I fold to a bet of $20. Stack: $403.

199. K2o (sb). I fold to raises, first to $6 and then to $18. Stack: $401.

200. KQo. Four call, I raise to $20 and win the pot. Stack: $417.

201. KTs. Two call, I raise to $15 and win the pot. Stack: $427.

202. 32o. Fold. Stack: $427.

203. 74o. Fold. Stack: $427.

204. A2o (bb). Four, including me, see the flop. Flop is A43. All check. Turn is an 8; I bet $15 and win the pot. Stack: $434.

205. AJo (sb). I call and four see a flop of TT3. I check and fold to a bet of $15. Stack: $431.

206. 43o. Fold. Stack: $431.

207. 82o. Fold. Stack: $431.

208. 32o. Fold. Stack: $431.

209. 87o. Fold. Stack: $431.

210. 42s. Fold. Stack: $431.

211. T2s (bb). I fold to a pre-flop raise to $15. Stack: $428.

212. K9s (sb). I call and six see the flop of A53. I check and fold to a bet of $15. Stack: $425.

213. 94o. Fold. Stack: $425.

214. Q3s. Fold. Stack: $425.

215. KK. I raise to $15 and take the pot. Stack: $435.

216. AJs. I raise ($18) a limper and win the pot. Stack: $445.

217. Q2o. Fold. Stack: $445.

218. KTo (bb). I check and five see a flop of A88. I fold to a bet of $15. Stack: $442.

219. 83o (sb). Fold. Stack: $440.

220. A4s. I fold to a pre-flop raise to $12. Stack: $440.

221. QJs. I call but then fold to a raise to $20. Stack: $437.

222. 94o. Fold. Stack: $437.

223. JJ (bb). There is a raise to 20 with one caller. I re-raise to $100. The original raiser, who has been at our table for four hands, goes all-in for $107 and has AA (the other player folds). An ace on the turn and I lose the hand. Stack: $330.

224. 63o (sb). Fold. Stack: $328.

225. 96o. Fold. Stack: $328.

226. J8o. Fold. Stack: $328.

227. Q3o. Fold. Stack: $328.

228. T9s. Fold. Stack: $328.

229. J3s. Fold. Stack: $328.

230. 72o (bb). I fold to pre-flop raises to $6 and then $26. Stack: $325.

231. A5o (sb). I call, and seven see a flop of A43. All check. Turn is K. I bet $10, all fold. Stack: $343.

232. 55. I call, and six see a flop of K42. I fold to a bet of $10. Stack: $340.

233. KQs. There are two callers in front of me. I raise to $25 and win the pot. Stack: $350.

234. T3s. Fold. Stack: $350.

235. 72o. Fold. Stack: $350.

236. A4o. Fold. Stack: $350.

237. 66 (bb). I check and five see a flop of J74. I check, but there is a bet of $20. I fold. Stack: $347.

238. AQs (sb). I fold to a raise to $22. Stack: $345.

239. T9o. Fold. Stack: $345.

240. J4o. Fold. Stack: $345.

241. Q3o. Fold. Stack: $345.

242. QQ. I call, another player raises to $10; I re-raise to $40 and win the pot. Stack: $362.

243. J5s (bb). I check, and five see a flop of AQ6. There is a bet of $15 and I fold. Stack: $359.

244. 92o (sb). I fold to a raise to $6. Stack: $357.

245. T9o. Fold. Stack: $357.

246. J3s. Fold. Stack: $357.

247. K6o. Fold. Stack: $357.

248. AKo. I raise to $25, the bb calls. The flop is QQ5; we both check. The turn is an 8. The bb checks, I bet $35 and the bb folds. Stack: $379.

249. T3o. Fold. Stack: $379.

250. 63o (bb). I check, and four see a flop of 954. I check and fold to a bet of $23. Stack: $376.

251. 86o (sb). Fold. Stack: $374.

252. T3o. Fold. Stack: $374.

253. Q8o. Fold. Stack: $374.

254. 64s. Fold. Stack: $374.

255. T4o. Fold. Stack: $374.

256. 66. I fold to a pre-flop raise to $15 followed by a re-raise to $45. Stack: $374.

257. 76o. Fold. Stack: $374.

258. Q7o (bb). I check, and four see a flop of T85. I fold to a bet of $10. Stack: $371.

259. 52o (sb). Fold. Stack: $369.

260. T9s. I fold to a pre-flop raise to $20. Stack: $369.

261. T3o. Fold. Stack: $369.

262. 92o. Fold. Stack: $369.

263. K8o. Fold. Stack: $369.

264. 74o. Fold. Stack: $369.

265. T9o (bb). I fold to a pre-flop raise to $6. Stack: $366.

266. KJo (sb). I fold to a pre-flop raise to $13. Stack: $364.

267. J2o. Fold. Stack: $364.

268. 86o. Fold. Stack: $364.

269. JTs. I raise ($26) five limpers and win the pot. Stack: $383.

270. Q3o. Fold. Stack: $383.

271. ATs (bb). I check and four see a flop of T87. I bet $5 (this bet should have been larger; however, as you will see it was a good thing it wasn't) and everyone calls. The turn is a 2. I check, and the next player bets $40 and is called by one of the other players (I fold). The two players hold JJ and 87. A jack on the river and both players rush to put their chips in the pot. My $5 bet, a "testing the water bet," did give me information: I knew that I was in, at best, third place on the hand. Stack: $375.

272. 63o (sb). Fold. Stack: $373.

273. J6o. Fold. Stack: $373.

274. J9o. Fold. Stack: $373.

275. 42o. Fold. Stack: $373.

276. 87o. Fold. Stack: $373.

277. 93o. Fold. Stack: $373.

278. 86o. Fold. Stack: $373.

279. 92o. Fold. Stack $373. I cash out and win, for the day, $173.

Here are some statistics regarding this session:

Total Hands Played: 279 (100.00%)

Total Hands Involved In: 59 (21.15%)

Total Hands Won: 28 (10.04%)

Here are some tables with more detailed statistics:

Table 1: Hands Played by Position and Betting

	Call Unraised Pot	Call Raised Pot	Raise Unraised Pot	Raise a Raised Pot	Call, then Fold to Raise	Raise and Fold to a Re-raise	Raise and Call a Re-Raise	Call, Then Re-Raise a Raise	Totals
Big Blind	13	3	1	4		1			**22**
Small Blind	5	1		1	3		1		**11**
UTG			3					1	**4**
Button	2		4						**6**
Cut-Off			2		1				**3**
All Others	4		6	3			1		**14**
Totals	**24**	**4**	**16**	**8**	**4**	**1**	**2**	**1**	**60**

Table 2: Hands Won by Position and Betting

	Call Unraised Pot	Call Raised Pot	Raise	Raise a Raised Pot	Call, then Fold to Raise	Raise and Fold to a Re-raise	Raise and Call a Re-Raise	Call, Then Re-Raise a Raise	**Totals**
Big Blind	3	2	1	2		0			**8**
Small Blind	2	0		1	0		0		**3**
UTG			3					1	**4**
Button	0		4						**4**
Cut-Off			2		0				**2**
All Others	0		6	2			0		**8**
Totals	**5**	**2**	**16**	**5**	**0**	**0**	**0**	**1**	**29**

Table 3: Percentage of Hands Won by Position and Betting.

	Call Unraised Pot	Call Raised Pot	Raise Unraised Pot	Raise a Raised Pot	Call, then Fold to Raise	Raise and Fold to a Re-raise	Raise and Call a Re-Raise	Call, Then Re-Raise a Raise	**Totals**
Big Blind	23%	67%	100%	50%		0%			**36%**
Small Blind	40%	0%		100%	0%		0%		**27%**
UTG			100%					100%	**100%**
Button	0%		100%						**67%**
Cut-Off			100%		0%				**67%**
All Others	0%		100%	67%			0%		**57%**
Totals	**21%**	**50%**	**100%**	**63%**	**0%**	**0%**	**0%**	**100%**	**48%**

Table 4: Hand Statistics

Hand	Actual # of Holdings	Expected # of Holdings	Variance	# of Hands Played	# of Hands Won	% of Hands Played	% of Hands Won
AA	0	1.26	(1.26)				
AK	4	3.37	0.63	4	3	100%	75%
AQ	6	3.37	2.63	5	2	83%	40%
AJ	4	3.37	0.63	2	1	50%	50%
AT	4	3.37	0.63	2	1	50%	50%
A9	2	3.37	(1.37)	0		0%	
A8	0	3.37	(3.37)				
A7	0	3.37	(3.37)				
A6	1	3.37	(2.37)	0		0%	
A5	1	3.37	(2.37)	1	1	100%	100%
A4	2	3.37	(1.37)	0		0%	
A3	0	3.37	(3.37)				
A2	8	3.37	4.63	2	1	25%	50%
KK	5	1.26	3.74	5	5	100%	100%
KQ	3	3.37	(0.37)	2	2	67%	100%
KJ	3	3.37	(0.37)	1	0	33%	0%
KT	3	3.37	(0.37)	2	1	67%	50%
K9	5	3.37	1.63	2	0	40%	0%
K8	5	3.37	1.63	0		0%	
K7	1	3.37	(2.37)	0		0%	
K6	4	3.37	0.63	0		0%	
K5	4	3.37	0.63	0		0%	
K4	1	3.37	(2.37)	0		0%	
K3	3	3.37	(0.37)	0		0%	

Table 4: Hand Statistics

Hand	Actual # of Holdings	Expected # of Holdings	Variance	# of Hands Played	# of Hands Won	% of Hands Played	% of Hands Won
K2	2	3.37	(1.37)	0		0%	
QQ	4	1.26	2.74	4	3	100%	75%
QJ	3	3.37	(0.37)	2	1	67%	50%
QT	3	3.37	(0.37)	1	1	33%	100%
Q9	1	3.37	(2.37)	0		0%	
Q8	2	3.37	(1.37)	0		0%	
Q7	1	3.37	(2.37)	1	0	100%	0%
Q6	2	3.37	(1.37)	0		0%	
Q5	1	3.37	(2.37)	0		0%	
Q4	4	3.37	0.63	2	0	50%	0%
Q3	6	3.37	2.63	0		0%	
Q2	2	3.37	(1.37)	0		0%	
JJ	2	1.26	0.74	2	1	100%	50%
JT	5	3.37	1.63	1	1	20%	100%
J9	3	3.37	(0.37)	0		0%	
J8	2	3.37	(1.37)	0		0%	
J7	4	3.37	0.63	0		0%	
J6	4	3.37	0.63	0		0%	
J5	2	3.37	(1.37)	1	0	50%	0%
J4	2	3.37	(1.37)	0		0%	
J3	4	3.37	0.63	0		0%	
J2	5	3.37	1.63	0		0%	
TT	1	1.26	(0.26)	1	1	100%	100%
T9	5	3.37	1.63	0		0%	

Table 4: Hand Statistics

Hand	Actual # of Holdings	Expected # of Holdings	Variance	# of Hands Played	# of Hands Won	% of Hands Played	% of Hands Won
T8	1	3.37	(2.37)	0		0%	
T7	4	3.37	0.63	0		0%	
T6	2	3.37	(1.37)	0		0%	
T5	2	3.37	(1.37)	0		0%	
T4	3	3.37	(0.37)	0		0%	
T3	8	3.37	4.63	0		0%	
T2	2	3.37	(1.37)	0		0%	
99	1	1.26	(0.26)	1	0	100%	0%
98	4	3.37	0.63	0		0%	
97	3	3.37	(0.37)	2	0	67%	0%
96	3	3.37	(0.37)	0		0%	
95	1	3.37	(2.37)	0		0%	
94	3	3.37	(0.37)	1	1	33%	100%
93	2	3.37	(1.37)	0		0%	
92	6	3.37	2.63	0		0%	
88	0	1.26	(1.26)				
87	5	3.37	1.63	1	1	20%	100%
86	5	3.37	1.63	0		0%	
85	2	3.37	(1.37)	0		0%	
84	5	3.37	1.63	0		0%	
83	3	3.37	(0.37)	0		0%	
82	3	3.37	(0.37)	0		0%	
77	1	1.26	(0.26)	1	0	100%	0%
76	4	3.37	0.63	1	0	25%	0%

Table 4: Hand Statistics

Hand	Actual # of Holdings	Expected # of Holdings	Variance	# of Hands Played	# of Hands Won	% of Hands Played	% of Hands Won
75	3	3.37	(0.37)	0		0%	
74	5	3.37	1.63	0		0%	
73	1	3.37	(2.37)	0		0%	
72	4	3.37	0.63	0		0%	
66	4	1.26	2.74	2	0	50%	0%
65	3	3.37	(0.37)	2	0	67%	0%
64	6	3.37	2.63	0		0%	
63	7	3.37	3.63	1	0	14%	0%
62	0	3.37	(3.37)				
55	1	1.26	(0.26)	1	0	100%	0%
54	2	3.37	(1.37)	0		0%	
53	5	3.37	1.63	0		0%	
52	4	3.37	0.63	0		0%	
44	0	1.26	(1.26)				
43	5	3.37	1.63	1	0	20%	0%
42	8	3.37	4.63	0		0%	
33	3	1.26	1.74	3	2	100%	67%
32	6	3.37	2.63	0		0%	
22	0	1.26	(1.26)				
Totals	279	279.24*	(0.24)*	60	29	22%	48%

*Difference is rounding error.

Table 5: Some Specific Types of Hands

Hand	Actual # of Holdings	Expected # of Holdings	Variance	# of Hands Played	# of Hands Won	% of Hands Played	% of Hands Won
Any Pair	22	16.38	5.62	20	12	91%	60%
Premium Hands*	22	13.04	8.96	21	15	95%	71%
Rule of 13 Hands**	30	23.59	6.41	2	1	7%	50%
Any Ace	32	41.70	(9.70)	16	9	50%	56%

*Premium hands are AA, AK, AQ, KK, QQ, JJ, and TT
**Rule of 13 Hands are defined on page 56 in Chapter 5

Further Reading

T
he number of available books on poker is skyrocketing. Many of these books are worthwhile; others, regretfully, are not. Our view on books is that if we can obtain *at least* two good ideas from a book, than the book is worth purchasing. All of the books and most of the software mentioned here can be purchased at bookstores specializing in poker and gambling, including ConJelCo (www.conjelco.com).

One of our favorite books is Roy West's *7 Card Stud: The Complete Course in Winning at Medium and Lower Limits*. Now this book is intended (obviously) for seven-card stud. However, his "Course Lesson 2: Poker is a People Game," and "Course Lesson 4: Reading Hands" are worth the price of the book by themselves. Now if you happen to want to play stud, then this book should shoot to the top of your list. But even if you don't ever want to hit a stud table, you should eventually read this book.

If you're just starting out playing limit hold'em, we consider six other books to be essential. Lou Krieger has written two excellent introductory books on hold'em: *Hold'em Excellence: From Beginner to Winner* and *More Hold'em Excellence: A Winner for Life*. Gary Carson's *The Complete Book of Hold'em Poker* is one of the best all-around introductions to hold'em and playing limit poker. David Sklansky and Mason Malmuth have written what many players consider to be the bible of limit hold'em: *Hold'em Poker for Advanced Players: 21st Century Edition*. Because many of your opponents will play exactly how the book suggests, we consider this work essential. Phil Gordon has penned an excellent overall introduction to poker: *Poker: The Real Deal*. Finally, Lee Jones's *Winning Low Limit Hold'em* is a superb guide to playing limit hold'em at the low limits. Several of his principles transfer to no-limit hold'em.

If you have a desire to play in an unlimited buy-in no-limit hold'em game, you must read *Pot-Limit & No-Limit Poker* by Stewart Reuben & Bob Ciaffone. In our view, this is the best book on the subject. If the tournament bug strikes you, a good introductory book on no-limit hold'em tournaments is *Championship No-Limit & Pot-Limit Hold'em* by T.J. Cloutier with Tom McEvoy. Ken Buntjer's *The Secret to Winning Big in Tournament Poker* gives a good framework into tournament play (though the focus is on limit hold'em).

Mike Caro supposedly will be coming out with a new edition of his classic, *The Body Language of Poker: Mike Caro's Book of Tells*. If he does, buy the new edition. If he doesn't, get a copy of the old one. This book has paid for itself many times over for the authors. David Sklansky's *The Theory of Poker* is not an easy read. But much of the material in this book is excellent, especially the fundamental theorem of poker; we strongly recommend it. Finally, Alan Schoonmaker develops the player grid more fully than we do in *The Psychology of Poker*. His hand reading section is another reason to read his book.

Shut Up and Deal is Jesse May's autobiographical novel. It's an excellent read, though it is unlikely to improve your game. Michael Wiesenberg's *The Official Dictionary of Poker* defines every poker term you could think of.

There are two computer software programs that we consider essential for everyone and two other programs for specific situations. First, go to www.brecware.com/Software/software.html and download Steve Brecher's *Hold'em Show-*

down. This program computes the odds for hand confrontations and is a wonderful tool. And you can't complain about the price: it's free. There are versions for both the Mac and Windows.

You will have to purchase the other essential piece of software: Mike Caro's *Poker Probe*. This is a DOS-based simulation tool useful when taking one hand (e.g. A♦A♥) and seeing what your odds are versus multiple callers.

If you play on the Internet, you should consider purchasing Poker Tracker (available at www.pokertracker.com). This software allows you to download hands, learn about your betting patterns, your opponent's patterns, and much more. We highly recommend it.

Finally, if you're not keeping track of your results (with a diary), there is software available that does the job. One excellent package is ConJelCo's *StatKing*. This Windows-based package allows you to calculate you win rate, confidence, standard deviation and a lot more.

Bibliography

Buntjer, Ken. *The Secret to Winning Big in Tournament Poker*. Milwaukie, OR: Red Rose Publishing, 1994.

Caro, Mike. *The Body Language of Poker: Mike Caro's Book of Tells*. Secaucus, NJ: Carol Publishing Group, 1984.

Carson, Gary. *The Complete Book of Hold'em Poker*. New York: Kensington Publishing Group, 2001.

Ciaffone, Bob and Stewart Reuben. *Pot-Limit & No-Limit Poker*. Self-published. 1997.

Cloutier, T.J. with Tom McEvoy. *Championship No-Limit & Pot-Limit Hold'em*. Las Vegas: Cardsmith Publishing, 1997.

Gordon, Phil and Jonathan Grotenstein. *Poker: The Real Deal*. New York: Simon Spotlight Entertainment, 2004.

Jones, Lee. *Winning Low-Limit Hold'em*. Pittsburgh, PA: ConJelCo, 1994.

Krieger, Lou. *Hold'em Excellence: From Beginner to Winner*. Pittsburgh, PA: ConJelCo, 2000.

———. *More Hold'em Excellence: A Winner for Life*. Pittsburgh, PA: ConJelCo, 1999.

May, Jesse. *Shut Up and Deal*. New York: Doubleday, 1998.

Schoonmaker, Alan N., Ph.D. *The Psychology of Poker*. Henderson, NV: Two Plus Two Publishing, 2000.

Sklansky, David. *The Theory of Poker*. Las Vegas: Two Plus Two Publishing, 1994.

Sklansky, David and Mason Malmuth. *Hold'em Poker for Advanced Players: 21st Century Edition*. Henderson, NV: Two Plus Two Publishing, 1999.

West, Roy. *Seven-Card Stud: The Complete Course in Winning at Medium and Lower Limits*. Las Vegas: Poker Plus Publications, 1996.

Wiesenberg, Michael. *The Official Dictionary of Poker*. Inglewood, CA: Mike Caro University of Poker, 1999.

The Matrix Theory: Starting Hand Charts

On the following pages you will find five starting hand charts, one for each of the table positions we discussed in the book: Early, Middle, Late, Small Blind, and Big Blind. The left hand column of each chart indicates what the action is to you preflop. For example, *Raise/Call* means there has been a raise and one or more callers by the time it is your turn to act. The columns to the right indicate the various possible options you have with particular hands. So *Raise/Call/Fold* means that raising, calling or folding, may be appropriate with the hands listed in that column. The Occasional column means just that, these hands can be played occasionally, but are often tricky hands that require you to proceed with caution. Remember, the Matrix theory states that you must take multiple variables into account to determine what the best action may be at that time. These tables should only be used as a starting point; you must use your poker skills and opponent-reading skills to make the correct action.

Here is an example as to how to read the chart:

You are in the small blind with AQs, there have been two limpers to you. What should you do? First you go to Figure 4, Small Blind Starting Hands. Then you find the Multiple Limpers row. Move along that row until you find AQs. It is under the Raise/Call column, meaning based on your knowledge of the limpers ahead of you, the big blind behind you, and your own image at the table, you should either raise with hand or call with this hand.

Table 1: Early Position Starting Hands

	Raise	Raise/ Call	Raise/ Fold	Raise/ Call/ Fold	Call	Call/ Fold	Occasional
First In	AA-TT, AK, AQs				AQo	99-22	AJs
One Limper	AA-KK	QQ-99, AK		AQs		88-22	
Multiple Limpers	N/A						
Raise	AA-KK	AK		QQ-TT			
Raise/Call	N/A						
Limp/ Raise	N/A						
Raise/ Reraise	N/A						

Table 2: Middle Position Starting Hands

	Raise	Raise/Call	Raise/Fold	Raise/Call/Fold	Call	Call/Fold	Occasional
First In	AA-88, AK-AQ				AQo	77-22	AJs
One Limper	AA-KK	QQ-99, AK				88-22	KQs, AJ
Multiple Limpers	AA-TT, AK-AQ	99-22					KQs
Raise	AA-KK	AK		QQ-TT			99-77
Raise/Call	AA-KK			QQ-JJ, AK		TT-55	
Limp/ Raise	AA-KK			QQ-TT, AK-AQ		99-55	
Raise/ Reraise	AA		KK	QQ			

Table 3: Late Position Starting Hands

	Raise	Raise/ Call	Raise/ Fold	Raise/ Call/Fold	Call	Call/ Fold	Occasional
First In	AA-22, AK-A9, KQ-KT, QJ-QT		JTs-32s				A8-A2
One Limper	AA-QQ, AK		JJ-22, AQ-AT, T9s-32s	KQ-KT, QJ-QT, JT			
Multiple Limpers	AA-QQ, AK-AQ	JJ-99	AJ-AT	KQs-KTs, QJs, QTs, JTs, 98s-65s	88-22		
Raise	AA-KK	AK	AQ	QQ-55			
Raise/Call	AA-KK			QQ-TT, AK		99-55, AQs-AJs	
Limp/ Raise	AA-KK			QQ-55, AK-AQ, AJs			
Raise/ Reraise	AA-KK			QQ-JJ			

Table 4: Small Blind Starting Hands

	Raise	Raise/Call	Raise/Fold	Raise/Call/Fold	Call	Occasional
First In	AA-77, AK-A9, KQ-KT, QJ-QT	66-22, A8-A2, KQ-K9, QJ-Q9, JT-J9		Any other 1-gap, or 2-cap hands	All other connectors	
One Limper	AA-QQ, AK-AQ		JJ-22	KQ-KT, QJ-QT, JT	AJ-AT, KQ-KJ, T9s-32s	
Multiple Limpers	AA-QQ, AK	JJ-22, AQ		KQs-KTs, QJs, QTs , JTs	88-22, AJ-AT, 98s-32s, KQo-76o, KJo-J9o	
Raise	AA-KK	AK		QQ-TT		99-77
Raise/Call	AA-KK	AK			QQ-JJ	
Limp/Raise	AA-KK	AK	-		QQ-JJ	-
Raise/ Reraise	AA		-	KK-QQ		

Table 5: Big Blind Starting Hands

	Raise	Raise/Call	Raise/Call/Fold	Call	Occasional
First In	Not applicable				
One Limper	AA-99, AK-AQ, AJs			Everything else	
Multiple Limpers	AA-QQ, AK			Everything else	
Raise	AA-KK	AK	QQ-TT	-	99-77
Raise/Call	AA-KK	AK	QQ-JJ	-	
Limp/Raise	AA-KK	AK		QQ-JJ	TT
Raise/Reraise	AA		KK-QQ		

Glossary

This appendix provides definitions of common poker terms and terms used in this book. This is by no means a complete list of poker terminology; for a more complete listing you may wish to look at Michael Wiesenberg's *Poker Dictionary*.

Aggressive: A player that normally enters a pot with a raise (or re-raise). An aggressive player usually bets the flop and takes the lead in the betting.

Back Door: Completing a hand (usually a straight or flush) by hitting two running cards.

Bad Beat: When a player loses a hand that he should have won when a large statistical favorite. For example, if a player holding A♣A♠ goes all-in pre-flop and faces an opponent holding 7♠2♣ but loses, he has suffered a bad beat. Bad beats are statistical anomalies.

Big Blind: The second of the two forced bets in hold'em and other "flop" games. In a game with $1 and $2 blinds, the "$2" refers to the big blind.

Blinds: The two forced bets pre-flop to induce action in hold'em and other "flop" games. A few no-limit hold'em games are played with *three* blinds: a small blind immediately following the button, a big blind in the next seat, and a small blind on the button.

Bluff: Betting with a hand that is not a winning hand in an attempt to take the pot from better hands. In order for a pure bluff to work, all other hands must fold. (See also *semibluff*.)

Board: The five *community cards* in hold'em and other flop games.

Button: The white plastic disk usually marked "Dealer" that moves around the table in a clockwise direction. The button signifies the position of the theoretical dealer, and gives that player the benefit of acting last on every round of betting except pre-flop.

Buy-in: The amount of chips you purchase to start a game. Many of the no-limit games described in this book have fixed buy-ins of $100 or $200. Other games have a range of allowed buy-ins (for example, from $200 to $500). Most card rooms also enforce a minimum buy-in.

Calling Station: A player that will call almost any bet or raise. This type of player, when he plays a hand, believes that he almost always holds the best hand, or that he has a decent chance to draw out to win the pot. Bluffing a calling station is suicidal.

Coin-toss: When two hands with approximately the same chance of winning the pot face each other in an all-in situation. The most common coin-toss situation is when a pair faces two overcards.

Community Cards: The five *board* cards that all players share in hold'em and other *flop* games.

Completing the Rainbow: When the *board* has a *rainbow flop*, if the *turn* card is from the fourth suit, the turn is said to "complete the rainbow."

Cutoff: The player sitting to the right of the *button*. This player is referred to as the cutoff or as sitting in the cutoff position or cutoff seat.

Draw: A hand that needs typically one more card in order to become a made hand. For example, a player holding

8♥6♥ and looking at a board of Q♥J♥4♣ would have a flush draw.

Drop: Another word for the house's share of a poker game (see also *rake*). In California, where variable rakes are prohibited, the house drop is typically $3 on the flop.

Early Position: The first three people to act after the *blinds* in a full ten-handed game.

Expected Value (EV): The amount of money you would expect to win (or lose) by making any specific action. Expected value is tied to *pot odds*.

Flat Betting: When a player bets the exact same amount on all the betting rounds.

Heads-up: When there are specifically two players battling for a pot.

Hole Cards: The two cards a player is dealt in hold'em.

Idiot-end: The low end of a straight. For example, if a player holds 2♥3♣ and the board is Q♦6♠4♥/K♥/5♣, he has the idiot-end of the straight.

Image: How your opponents view your play. You could be described as *tight, loose, aggressive, passive, calling station, maniac,* and other terms.

Kicker: The second card in a player's hole cards. If a player holds A♣9♠, he has an ace with a 9 *kicker*. If the flop comes with a 9, the player would have a pair of nines with an ace kicker.

Late Position: The last three people to act before the *blinds* act in a full ten-handed game.

Lead: A player that will normally bet; that is, take the initiative on hands that he is involved in.

Leading the Flock: When one player's actions cause the next players to make the same action, the first player is said to have "lead the flock."

Limp: A player *limps* (into the pot) when he just calls the *big blind*. Limping occurs only before the *flop*.

Loose: A player that plays more hands than the average player is considered *loose*.

Made Hand: When a player completes a straight, flush, or a higher hand, he has a *made hand* and is no longer drawing to complete a hand.

Maniac: A player who plays far too many hands, usually raising most hands that he plays. For a maniac, often any two cards will do. An extreme case of a maniac is one who bets and raises at any given opportunity from start to finish on almost every hand.

Middle Position: The fourth through sixth people to act following the *blinds* in a full ten-handed game.

Nuts: The best possible hand, given the *board*. If the board were Q♣Q♠7♥/6♥/A♦, a player holding Q♦Q♥ would hold the nuts.

Offsuit: When a player's *hole cards* are of two different suits (e.g. 7♠4♣), his cards are offsuit. This hand can be written as 74o.

One-gap Hands: When a player's *hole cards* are numerically two spots from each other. Examples include QT, T8, and 64.

The Option: In an unraised hand, the *big blind* has the *option* to raise or check before the *flop*. If other players have posted *big blinds* (this occurs when they sit out hands), they, too, will have an option to raise.

Orbit: One round of a *flop* game, so that each player has been in every position (*blinds*, *button*, early and late).

Passive: A player that normally just checks or calls and rarely *leads* at hands.

Pocket Pair: If a player's *hole cards* are a pair, he has a *pocket pair*.

Position: When a player acts in a hand of no-limit hold'em and other *flop* games. A player's *physical position* is his when he acts pre-*flop* (see *early position, middle position,* and *late position*). A player's *relative position* is when he acts in betting rounds after the *flop*.

Premium Hand: A hand that is almost always playable pre-*flop*. Aces and kings are *premium hands*; queens, jacks, and ace-king may be *premium hands*.

Rainbow: A *flop* of three different suits, for example, T♣8♥8♦.

Rake: The money the house (casino or cardroom) takes from the pot for running the game. In many locations, this is stated as "10% up to $3." In other locations, such as California, a variable *rake* is prohibited and the *drop* might be, for example, $3 on the *flop*.

River: The fifth and final *board* or *community* card.

Run Over: Force opponents out of a pot by making large bets.

Running Cards: Cards that follow. For hold'em, this refers to the next *board* card(s).

Semi-bluff: Betting with a *drawing* hand that would not normally bet in order to drive out your opponents but, if called, still has a chance of winning the pot.

Set: Three of a kind, with a player holding a pair and another card of his pair is on the board. For example, if a player holds 7♣7♠, and the flop comes Q♦7♦3♥, he has flopped a set of sevens. (This should not be confused with trips, when a player holds one card of a rank and there are two more of that rank on the board. If the player holds A♦7♣ and the flop comes 7♥7♠3♣, the player has flopped trips.)

Small Blind: The first of two forced bets in hold'em and other "flop" games. In a $1/$2 *blinds* $100 fixed buy-in no-limit hold'em game, the "$1" refers to the *small blind*.

Slow-playing: When a player who holds a big hand either underbets or checks his hand, he is said to be slow-playing. For example, if a player holds A♣A♠ and just *limps* pre-*flop*, he has slow-played his hand.

Stack Off: When a player moves all-in, and is called, he has "stacked off" against his opponents.

Stack Size: The amount of chips a player holds. Having a large *stack size* affords players additional options, including intimidation plays.

Standard Raise: The raise that most players use when raising pre-*flop*. While each game usually has such a raise, it can (and does) vary widely among games depending on chip stacks, the players, and other factors.

Stealing the Blinds: Raising with a hand that you would normally fold in an attempt to win the *blinds*.

Stone-Cold Nuts: If a player has a hand that cannot be beaten no matter what future board card comes, he has the stone-cold nuts. For example, if the *flop* and *turn* are T♥2♦3♥/T♣, and a player holds T♠T♦, he has the stone cold nuts.

Suited Cards: When a player's *hole cards* are of the same suit (e.g. T♠3♠), they are *suited cards*. Such cards are often referred to simply as *suited*. The example hand can also be written as T3s.

Suited Connectors: A player holds *suited connectors* as his *hole* cards when his cards are of the same suit and are adjacent to each other in rank. Examples include Q♦J♦, T♠9♠, and 4♣3♣.

Tell: A physical or verbal action by a player that gives another player an indication of the cards he holds.

Tight: A player that plays fewer hands than the average player is considered *tight*.

Tilt: A player that makes bad plays that are generally induced by a recent *beat*, string of *beats*, or other negative factors is said to be on *tilt*.

Turn: The fourth *board* or *community* card.

Two-gap Hands: When a player's *hole cards* are numerically three spots from each other. Examples include Q9, T7, and 63.

Under the Gun: The first player to act following the *blinds* pre-*flop*. This is abbreviated as "UTG."

Wheel: The lowest possible straight, ace through five.

Index

About the Authors

Russell Fox began playing poker while in college at Berkeley but did not begin to take the game seriously until 1999. Then, while living in Seattle with free time, he began to play in the local cardrooms and tournaments. Almost immediately he became a winning player, and he has not had a losing year to date. He has had numerous final table appearances, including winning the 2001 BARGE no-limit hold'em championship. You can usually find Russ playing no-limit hold'em in one of the Southern California cardrooms.

Away from the tables, Russ is an Enrolled Agent (a Federally licensed tax preparer) and the principal of his own consulting and tax practice, Clayton Financial and Tax. He also has written articles for two poker websites, www.pokerschoolonline.com and www.thepokerforum.com.

Russ's other interests including bicycling and tournament bridge. He resides in Irvine, California.

Scott T. Harker has also been playing poker since college. Poker became an outlet for his competitive juices. He began playing poker seriously to supplement his income while living in Las Vegas. Today Scott plays mainly online poker, in low-to-middle-limit and no-limit hold'em cash games. Scott has been a successful winning cash game player since 1999.

Scott has his own consulting practice, specializing in technical and business documentation. He is also an editor for ConJelCo, and a published poet.

Currently living in Youngstown, Ohio, Scott's other interests revolve around his family: his wife Brittania and his son Blaine.

About the Publisher

ConJelCo specializes in books and software for the serious gambler. In addition to this book, ConJelCo publishes *Winning Low-Limit Hold'em* by Lee Jones, *Hold'em Excellence: From Beginner to Winner* by Lou Krieger, *More Hold'em Excellence: A Winner for Life* by Lou Krieger, *Internet Poker: How to Play and Beat Online Poker Games*, by Lou Krieger and Kathleen Keller Watterson, *Winning Omaha/8 Poker* by Mark Tenner and Lou Krieger, *Serious Poker* by Dan Kimberg, *Stepping Up: The Recreational Player's Guide to Beating Casino and Internet Poker* by Randy Burgess, as well as *Video Poker—Optimum Play* by Dan Paymar. ConJelCo also publishes software including *Blackjack Trainer* for the Macintosh and Windows, *Ken Elliott's CrapSim* for DOS, and *StatKing* for Windows (record keeping software).

We periodically publish a newsletter sent free to our customers. *The Intelligent Gambler* carries articles by our authors as well as other respected authors in the gambling community. In addition, it is the source of information about new ConJelCo products and special offers.

We also sell books, software and videos from other publishers. If you'd like a free catalog or to be put on the mailing list for *The Intelligent Gambler* you can write to us at:

ConJelCo
1460 Bennington Ave.
Pittsburgh, PA 15217

Our phone number is 800-492-9210 (412-621-6040 outside of the U.S.), and our fax number is 412-621-6214.

ConJelCo, and its catalog, is on the Web at *http://www.conjelco.com* or e-mail us at *orders@conjelco.com*.